Face to Face With God

FACE TO FACE
WITH GOD

Moses, Eluma and Job

———

TREVOR DENNIS

First published in Great Britain in 1999
Society for Promoting Christian Knowledge
Holy Trinity Church
Marylebone Road
London NW1 4DU

British Library Cataloguing-in-Publication Data

A catalogue record for this book is available
from the British Library

ISBN 0–281–05203–4

Typeset by Wilmaset Ltd, Birkenhead, Wirral
Printed in Great Britain by
Arrowsmiths, Bristol

Contents

This book is dedicated with gratitude
to the memory of two remarkable women,
who, in their great old age,
were an inspiration to me,
and have remained so ever since,

Nora Atkin
and
Kitty Collinson

Preface

I have long wished to write something on the book of Job. It is a work of such dramatic power and beauty. No other work in the Bible looks at the face of human suffering for so long, or with such devastating honesty. No other work is so fearless and persistent in its questioning of the nature and character of God against the background of the tragedies and injustice to which human life is so often exposed. No other work asks with such determination whether human beings would not make a better job of looking after the earth. Nowhere else in the Bible are the attempts of religious people to give answers to those who are suffering subjected to such prolonged and fierce scrutiny. Nowhere else is their tendency to put their own religious convictions before the needs of those they are claiming to help so roundly condemned. And the vision of God that forms the climax of the work is surely one of the brightest in all Scripture. For years I have been enthralled with this work. The last chapter of this book has given me a chance to say some of what I wish to say about it.

When I wrote *Sarah Laughed: Women's Voices in the Old Testament* (SPCK, 1994), I was disappointed that I did not have room for the marvellously funny story of Manoah and his wife in Judges 13, the woman the rabbis came to call Eluma. This book has given me the chance to make a detailed study of that story, and I have found it even more intriguing and delightful than I expected.

But the chief surprise of this book for me has been Moses. Until I came to work on the stories of his encounters with God for the first four chapters of this volume, I had not quite realized the stature of the man as he is portrayed, nor the extraordinary depth and closeness of relationship with God that is expressed. These are inspiring stories, sometimes disquieting, but always challenging, and of great significance for contemporary spirituality, not just, of course, within the Christian Church.

I wrote this book, like my last one, *Looking God in the Eye*, by putting writing weeks into my diary, and then keeping them as clear as possible of my general duties here at Chester Cathedral. I am grateful to my colleagues on the Chapter, Stephen Smalley, Michael Rees, Owen Conway, and James Newcome for their patience with me and their support.

I owe a great deal, also, to the staff of SPCK, particularly Lucy Gasson, with whom I first discussed these chapters, Robin Keeley, who took over from her as Editor, and David Sanders, the copy editor. They have been unfailing in their kindness and their encouragement. The encouragement and the love of Caroline, my wife, and our children, Eleanor, Sarah, Joanna, and Timothy have inevitably meant the most to me. If over the years I have remained human, or even developed my humanity, then I have them to thank for it before anyone else.

Yet, of course, others have been an inspiration to me and have had a profound influence upon me. One of them is Nora Atkin, who was Caroline's godmother. We used to visit her as a family in her great old age, when she was confined to her upstairs flat and spent most of her time in a wheel chair. On one occasion, when she was well into her nineties, I discovered her reading Teilhard de Chardin's *The Phenomenon of Man* (a difficult book by any standards), and finding it 'very interesting'. She was a quite remarkable person, and we all loved her. This book is dedicated to her memory.

It is also dedicated to the memory of Kitty Collinson. When we moved to Salisbury in 1982, we inherited Kitty as our baby-sitter. Very soon she became a member of the family. She was already in her eighties, but she had the spirit, the mischief, the sheer zest for living of a young person, as well as an always enquiring mind, a huge sense of fun, and a profound faith. Two weeks after we finally left Salisbury at the end of 1993 she had a heart attack, and within a few days was dead. None of us will ever forget her. Both she and Nora would have

PREFACE

been so surprised to find their names on the dedication page of
this book, but I dare to hope they would have been pleased.

Trevor Dennis
Chester Cathedral

Introduction

This book comes as a sequel to *Looking God in the Eye*. That dealt with stories of encounter with God in Genesis. This is concerned with stories of encounter with God in Exodus, Numbers, Deuteronomy, Judges, and Job.

It picks up where *Looking God in the Eye* left off. The subject of the last chapter of *Looking God in the Eye* was the Joseph story that takes up the last quarter of Genesis. Beyond Genesis, the first time God reappears on stage is at the start of Exodus 3, in the famous story of the Burning Bush. That story is explored in the first chapter of this book.

Moses is born in Exodus 2 and dies in Deuteronomy 34. No-one else in the Bible is the major human figure in such a long stretch of material. Even David's story is not as long as that, and the four Gospels put together do not amount to so many pages. However, the bulk of the second half of Exodus, the whole of Leviticus, and large parts of Numbers are devoted to the terms of the Torah, the teaching offered by God to his people to equip them for life in the Promised Land, and Deuteronomy is almost entirely given over to a rehearsal of the Torah for the benefit of the new generation born in the desert, just before they cross over the Jordan river. Thus the main 'character' in Exodus 20—Deuteronomy 31, apart from God himself, is not Moses, but the Torah. For chapter after chapter we hear God delivering it to Moses on the summit of Mount Sinai, and in Deuteronomy Moses spends almost all his time conveying it to the next generation. It is not his own teaching, but God's, and he is but the messenger boy. He does not draw attention to himself, but to the Torah and the God whose expression it is.

Yet still enough is said about Moses to turn him into a compelling figure, a hero who towers above any other human character we meet in the Old Testament. In particular there are several passages that trace the development of his relationship with God, and we will look closely at a few of those. After the Burning Bush perhaps the most significant is the episode of the Golden Calf in Exodus 32—3. Almost two chapters will be devoted to that, and the first of them will lead us to some passages in Numbers also. Before that we will explore the nature of Moses' prayer, and examine two very striking examples of it in Exodus 5 and Numbers 11. We will complete our discussion of him by considering briefly the account of his death at the end of Deuteronomy.

We will seek to enter as deeply as we can into these stories, see how they are written, and how both Moses and God are portrayed. From time to time we will comment upon their possible significance for us and for the contemporary Church. We will also stand back from them and ask some awkward questions, in particular about their theology, about what they have to say about God. If we are alarmed by what we find, we will have no hesitation in saying so.

Our final chapter will be devoted to the appearance of God to Job in the whirlwind in Job 38—42. We will not be able to go straight to what is the climax and conclusion of the book. We will need first to examine the Prologue to the work in some detail, and tell of a few things along the way beyond. In other words, we will have to set Job's encounter with God in its literary context. As a result that chapter of ours will be longer than the others, but we have divided it into manageable sections, so the task of reading it should not be unnecessarily daunting.

After Job 38—42 there can only be silence. Job himself is left speechless. The sheer beauty of the poetry, the depth and colour of the portrayal of God, the scale of the vision and the enormity of the questions addressed all conspire in the end to shut our mouths also. To proceed to another encounter with God after that would be to risk a sense of anti-climax.

But in between Moses and Job comes Eluma. Everyone who knows anything about the Bible at all has heard of Moses and Job. Many of those who are extremely familiar with it will be baffled by the name Eluma. That is because the name does not appear in the biblical text, but only in rabbinic commentaries. It is the name, or, to be more precise, one of the names, the rabbis have given to the wife of Manoah in Judges 13. There she is simply called 'the woman', or 'Manoah's wife'. Our penultimate chapter will be concerned with her tale, and we will explain in the course of it why we think it important not to leave her without a name, and why we gratefully received the rabbis' suggestion of 'Eluma'.

Eluma's story comes as some light relief after the pathos and the passion of the Moses stories, though we will find more humour in the Prologue to the book of Job. Judges 13 is comedy, delightful, mischievous, subversive comedy, told from beginning to end at Manoah's expense. Behind the text we ourselves hear women's voices and women's laughter, and suspect it may be one of those stories in the Old Testament which originated in women's circles. It is certainly highly significant as one of only three stories in the Old Testament concerned with direct encounter between God and women. The first two are those of the woman in the Garden of Eden and Hagar (Hagar has two separate meetings to describe), both of which we dealt with in *Looking God in the Eye*. Eluma's is the third and last, and we have to wait till Luke's story of the annunciation to Mary of Nazareth, or John's story of the meeting of Mary of Magdala and the risen Christ, before we come across anything similar.

Eluma's story, therefore, is of a rare importance, and could not have been ignored, even if we had wanted to pass it by. But its significance does not lie simply in its rarity and its humour. It is a profound tale, full of hope and grace. Set between the Moses stories and Job, it is not overawed by the company it keeps.

*   *   *

To make discussion easier, each of the chosen passages is translated afresh from the Hebrew, and indeed, whenever the biblical text is quoted, a new translation is offered.

One important matter to do with the translation needs to be explained. God is often called YHWH in the Old Testament. That came to be the name above all names that distinguished the God of ancient Israel from the deities of the surrounding peoples. Written Hebrew has no vowels, so the letters YHWH are all we find in the text. Over several centuries of our own Common Era, admittedly, various signs were developed in the form of dots and dashes placed above or below the letters, to indicate the vowel sounds that should be pronounced. But the name YHWH was considered too sacred to take on the lips, and the custom had long been established of readers saying 'Adonai', or 'the/my Lord' instead, whenever they came across it in the text. So the vowel signs for 'Adonai' were given to YHWH, to indicate that 'Adonai' should be the word actually spoken, producing something on the Hebrew page that is nearly as impossible to pronounce as YHWH is on ours.

Religious Jews would still discourage us from trying to pronounce the divine name, and they have more than custom to support their case. For our most intimate God is beyond description, and beyond naming. God is essentially the unnameable one, as we reminded ourselves in the chapter on Hagar in *Looking God in the Eye*. A name, therefore, that cannot be pronounced seems only too fitting. It tells both of God's closeness, for it suggests she has come out into the open and revealed her identity, yet it preserves the sense of his otherness, his being always beyond our grasp and our telling. Most English translations of the Bible follow Jewish custom and substitute 'the Lord' for YHWH. The Jerusalem Bible and the New Jerusalem Bible vocalize it as 'Yahweh'. For the reasons we have just outlined, and encouraged further by current scholarly convention, we have left YHWH as it is.

1

The Fire of God, and Much Talk

(Exodus 3.1—4.17)

We come first to Moses, and to one of the most famous passages in all Scripture, the story of the Burning Bush. It is a long passage, and almost all of it is talk. That is how it will be from this point on with God and Moses. 'Moses is so often addressed by God,' says James Nohrnberg,[1] 'that it is almost his calling to be called.'

But we have more than God's speaking here. We have dialogue. The balance is different from that of the remarkable dialogue between Abraham and God in Genesis 18, where Abraham did most of the talking. Here God will have the long speeches, and Moses will only be able to punctuate them with brief interventions.

The course of Moses' life will be altered irrevocably by this meeting, and, as we will see in our next chapter, when we go beyond the dialogue to the beginning of his second one with God (see 5.22–3), he himself will be transformed by it. God will be also. At first we might think he is largely unchanged. This is not another Flood story; it does not alter the way in which he will continue to live with human beings. There will be no dramatic shift in his focus, as Abraham brought him to, for a time at least, when he was contemplating the destruction of Sodom. Nor will he go away bearing another name, as he did after his first encounter with Hagar. He will certainly emerge more angry than when he began. Beyond that he will seem the same as he was in the beginning, with the same vision of things, the same preoccupation with his people's plight, the same determination to come to their rescue. Yet, just as the change in Moses only becomes apparent beyond the passage, so the more profound changes for God will only be revealed as the story of the rescue from Egypt progresses.

1

Eventually God will know that at the Burning Bush he gained his closest friend. Moses will turn out to be his reliable fellow worker, on whom he will depend for large visions to take on reality. Moses will be his confidant, and will repay him with passionate plain-speaking. He will be able to speak with him 'face to face, as one speaks to a friend' (Exodus 33.11). After Moses God will have no-one so close to him, until the Gospels come to talk of Jesus of Nazareth. After the Burning Bush, life for God will never be the same again.

At the start of the story Moses is in Midian, looking after the flocks of his father-in-law, Jethro. He has escaped from Egypt, where his life was in danger from Pharaoh. The family of Jacob has become a people and, growing most wonderfully fast, has turned into a vast multitude that fills the land, just as God promised their ancestors they would. The trouble is, it is the wrong land. God means them to be in Canaan, as we well know from Genesis. Thanks to Joseph, they are in Egypt. When first Jacob and his sons settled there, again thanks to Joseph all was astonishingly well. But now a new ruler is in power who has no memory of Joseph and the way he saved his country from ruin. Driven by absurd paranoia this Pharaoh means to break the backs of Jacob's people. He tries forced labour, and then, when that fails, genocide. The people of Israel, the people now of the Holocaust, begins its life in Exodus under a ruler who tries to wipe it out. When it is newborn, in the first moments of its infancy, Pharaoh gives orders for its baby boys to be killed by their midwives or thrown into the Nile. Then, throttling and drowning; in our own century, asphyxiation in gas chambers, and being mowed down beside burial pits. The first chapter of Exodus has a prophetic irony about it that the author could not have dreamed of in his worst nightmares.

Moses himself escapes when he is born, thanks to the ingenuity of his mother, the close attentions of his sister, and the quite unexpected compassion of Pharaoh's daughter. Once weaned he is adopted by the princess and becomes a member of the royal household. He is now a cuckoo in Pharaoh's nest! But if that leads us to expect him to seize power when he comes to manhood, and drive the tyrant out, then we are disappointed.

The stories of the period in Egypt in Exodus 1—14 contain much that is deliciously implausible, but beneath them lies a frighteningly realistic picture of the brutal tyrant. Tyrants with the kinds of resources as were enjoyed by Pharaohs in Egypt are not so easy to overthrow. The second Pharaoh of Exodus 1—14 (the first one dies relatively early on), who is no better than his predecessor, will need all the strength of God to dislodge him. The best the young Moses can do is save one of his kinsmen from being beaten to death by an Egyptian overseer (Exodus 2.11–12), intervene the next day in a fight between two others of his kinsmen (2.13–14) and, after fleeing to Midian, rescue the daughters of Jethro from a gang of bullies among the local shepherds (2.15–19). Such deeds hint of heroism and go far beyond what many of us would be prepared to do, yet they do not get Moses' people very far. As Charles Isbell says of the episode in Midian, 'Thrashing some country shepherds who terrorize helpless maidens is one thing, but the *real* bully is still far away, still belching forth orders of death, still enslaving the "brothers" with whom Moses had once felt such solidarity.'[2]

Something has to be done. The screams of the Israelites reach the ears of God, and the moans of their slow dying (Exodus 2.23–5). Something must be done.

Moses is out for what he thinks is just another day's shepherding. God comes to disconcert him, and to give him more important work to do.

The beginning of their encounter does not lead us to expect the remarkable degree of intimacy that will eventually be established between them.

Moses was shepherding the flock of Jethro, his father-in-law, priest of Midian, and he drove the flock behind the desert, and came to the mountain of God, to Horeb.
The messenger of YHWH appeared to him in flame of fire, out of the middle of a bush. He saw, and look! the bush was burning with fire, but the bush was not being consumed! (Exodus 3.1–2)
Moses said, 'Let me turn aside, to see this great sight, why the bush is not burning up.' YHWH saw that he had turned

3

aside to see, and God called to him out of the middle of the bush. 'Moses! Moses!' he said.

He said, 'Here I am.'

He said, 'Come no closer! Take off your sandals from your feet, for the place on which you are standing, it is holy ground!' He said, 'I am the God of your father, the God of Abraham, the God of Isaac, the God of Jacob.'

Moses hid his face, for he was afraid to gaze upon God. (4–6)

Where are we? We are 'behind the desert', in the back of beyond. We are in mysterious country, beyond the edges of maps, beyond human knowledge, nearly beyond human imagining. We have entered upon the very mystery of God. We are at the mountain of God, the place called Horeb, or, elsewhere in the traditions, Sinai.

> Sinai is permanently out in the territories, with the feral creature, the bedouin, and the storm. Set apart, well-nigh empty, this extraterritorial space is almost perforce holy. If it cannot be inhabited, it cannot be profaned – it can be visited, but its only 'native' is one whose presence is wholly and starkly Other.[3]

Yet if we return to the edge of that equally mysterious Garden of Eden and see the cherubim guarding its entrance and the lightning fire of their whirling sword, we are at once reminded of a most familiar place, one, at least, we have heard a good deal about, the holy of holies, the innermost sanctuary of God's temple in Jerusalem.[4] So here, behind the desert, when we hear talk of holy ground and of sandals having to be removed, we think immediately of the mosque, temple, or gurdwara, where still shoes have to be removed before we can enter. The echoes of organized religion are clear. It is significant that hitherto in the Bible we have not heard the phrase 'holy ground'. The concept of the holy came to the surface of the text only once in Genesis, in God's 'hallowing' the seventh day of creation (2.3). What could be holier, we might ask, than Hagar's well at Beer-lahai-roi, where she saw God and gave him a new name (16.7–14), or the spot in the Wadi Jabbok where Jacob wrestled with God through the small hours of the night (32.22–32)? Yet they were not *pronounced* holy. There is a new formality here, which is a token of things to come. The religion which Moses will establish at Sinai for the people of God will be preoccupied with holiness. Sinai will be holy. Their God will be holy. They, his people, will be called to be holy. God will be surrounded by reverence and awe, hidden from the sight of ordinary mortals. So at least the traditions and the priests will present him. Later, in Jerusalem, only the priests of his temple will claim to be able to get close to him. They have already left their mark upon the telling of this tale. Moses is not a priest, and so must keep his distance.[5] No-one can see God and live, the priests will say. So once Moses knows who he is speaking to, he covers his face.

For the time being we seem worlds away from those earlier stories in Genesis. Yet see where God is hiding here! (It *is* God, of course. 'The messenger of the Lord' is again just a way of speaking, similar, as D. Moody points out,[6] to phrases such as 'the face of God', or 'the glory of God'.) God is in no fine temple, but in a bush of thorns! In ancient Egypt the goddess Nut was sometimes portrayed as a small tree, or the trunk of a tree.[7] Christians today will more readily be reminded of a stable at Bethlehem, where the surroundings were again so very ordinary, or of a crown of thorns, where the glory of God was again seen for what it was.

Here the glory of God takes the form of fire, fire that lives and moves, that flickers, bends and dances, that attracts and fascinates, and yet does not burn or destroy. The bush is not harmed but hallowed by this fire. Sixteen chapters later God will again come to Mount Sinai in fire (19.18). Before that he will lead his people out of Egypt hidden by night in a column of fire that will light up the darkness (13.21). One day in the temple in Jerusalem a fire burning continuously on the altar will signify the presence of God (Leviticus 6.12–13), and much later still, so Luke will tell us, tongues of fire will rest on the heads of the followers of Jesus of Nazareth, and signify another new era in the history of the people of God (Acts 2.3–4).

Moses is not frightened by this fire, nor by the first sound of God's voice, the calling of his name. Only once he knows who is speaking to him, is he overwhelmed. Before that there is only curiosity. It is like someone who bumps into the Queen, fails to recognize her, engages her in conversation, and then is overcome when she reveals who she is. Moses has seen the fire, so he has already looked upon God, and he has not been unnerved. But now suddenly he hides his face. Suddenly the reality, the closeness of God is too much to bear. It will not always be so. Soon after this passage is ended he will march into the presence of God without any by your leave, will look him straight in the eye and tell him in no uncertain terms what's what.

Or might it be that Moses is troubled by what he sees in the fire when he comes close to it? Elsewhere in the Old Testament writers speak of the 'furnace', or the 'iron-smelter' of Egypt, to indicate the agonies the people endured during their period of bondage (Deuteronomy 4.20; 1 Kings 8.51; Jeremiah 11.4). Does Moses look into the furnace and see his people in the flames? So some rabbinic commentators have suggested.[8] The text does not say so. The text does not lead us in that direction. But once we have discovered that brilliant and terrifying phrase in Deuteronomy and the rest, once we recall the crematoria of Auschwitz, the thought will not leave our heads.[9]

If, nevertheless, we wish to keep closer to the text, we might say that Moses sees in the middle of the bush the burning pain and anger of God, and the flames of his passion for justice. For this is how the passage continues:

> YHWH said, 'I have seen, oh yes, I have seen the misery of my people in Egypt, and I have heard their cries of anguish in the face of their slave-drivers. I tell you, I know their pain! I have come down to rescue them from Egypt's grasp, and to bring them up from that land to a land that is beautiful and spacious, to a land that is flowing with milk and honey, to the place of the Canaanite, the Hittite, the Amorite and the Perizzite, the Hivvite and the Jebusite. See, now, the cries of anguish of the children of Israel have reached me and I have seen the oppression with which Egypt oppresses them.
>
> 'Now go! I am sending you to Pharaoh. Bring my people, the children of Israel, out of Egypt!' (3.7–10)

6

THE FIRE OF GOD, AND MUCH TALK

A sting in the tail, if ever there was one! It is one thing for Moses
to be reminded of the sufferings of his people back in Egypt. It
is one thing, and a most comforting thing, to hear God promising that he will rescue them. It is quite another for Moses to
learn that God cannot achieve the rescue on his own, but needs
his help. It is one thing to hear the faint cries of the Israelites
echoing from the shoulders of the mountain of God, behind
the desert, far from the Egyptian border. It is quite another to
be told to go to the tyrant's palace and confront him with the
demand he stop his brutality. It is one thing to learn of Auschwitz. It is quite another to be ordered to go to Berlin and
engineer an end to the Holocaust.

Understandably, Moses does not feel equal to the task. His
authority has already been challenged, by one of his own
people back in Egypt. 'Who made you prince and judge over
us?' was the angry and defiant question of the man he tried to
stop fighting (2.14). Now he lets his cloak fall from his face.
The fear of going to Egypt is greater than any fear he now has
of looking upon God. He cannot face the Pharaoh, but he can
face his God.

> Moses said to God, 'Who am I that I should go to Pharaoh,
> that I should bring the children of Israel out of Egypt?'
>
> He said, 'I tell you, I will be there with you. And this shall be
> the sign for you that I am the one who has sent you: when
> you bring the people out of Egypt, you will serve God upon
> this mountain.'
>
> Moses said to God, 'Look, suppose I come to the children
> of Israel and say to them, "The God of your fathers has sent
> me to you," and they say to me, "What is his name?", what
> shall I say to them?'
>
> God said to Moses, 'I will be there as I will be there.' He
> said, 'Tell the children of Israel, "I-will-be-there has sent me
> to you."' (3.11–14)

In this whole episode of the Burning Bush Moses has seven
speeches. One, near the beginning, is, in the Hebrew, just one
word long: *'hinneni'*, 'Here I am.' His very first, when he turns
aside to see the bush, is a matter of him talking, or perhaps
thinking, to himself. The other five, all addressed to God, are

7

objections, attempts to avoid the terrifying task God is giving him.

The first of those five, 'Who am I that I should go to Pharaoh?', not only seems entirely reasonable, but is what other stories in the Old Testament would lead us to expect. When God calls upon Gideon to save the Israelite tribes from their Midianite enemies, he claims he does not have the right breeding (Judges 6.15). Isaiah cries out that he is not fit to be in the presence of God (Isaiah 6.5), and when God calls Jeremiah to be a prophet, Jeremiah tells him he does not know how to speak because he is only a boy (Jeremiah 1.6). Both Gideon and Jeremiah, like Moses, receive the assurance that God will be with them. Later in our passage, Moses will object, like Jeremiah, that he is no good at public speaking. God promises both of them that he will give them the words to say. Before our passage is ended Moses will have received two signs from God that he means what he says, and a promise of a third. Gideon is given two signs by God also (Judges 6.17–21, 36–40). There seems to be something of a pattern to these things. We might say etiquette almost demands, when people are given a great commission by God, that they protest. It is a sign of their respect both for God and for the size and nature of the task they are being asked to undertake. Yet no-one except Moses openly protests *five times*. Only Jonah is more persistent in resisting God's call. In the end Moses will exhaust God's patience.

The second of his objections does not look like one at first. 'Look, suppose I come to the children of Israel and say to them, "The God of your fathers has sent me to you," and they say to me, "What is his name?", what shall I say to them?' (3.13) It might seem a fair question, but who really wishes to know the answer? Is it really the Israelites, as Moses would have us and God believe, or is it Moses himself? Certainly, when Moses gets to Egypt, the only one who will ask about God's identity will be Pharaoh (5.2). If it is Moses who wants to know, as we begin to suspect, what is he after? Jacob also asked for God's name at the Jabbok, but he clearly needed to know. His assailant was truly a mysterious figure, and whether Jacob won or lost the wrestling bout might have depended on him discovering his identity. But already God has revealed himself to Moses as God, and as the God of his ancestors. Is Moses really intent on exploring deeper into the essential mystery of God, or is he just trying to wriggle out of going to Egypt? His other protests in the passage would suggest the second.

Certainly, God does not give a straight answer to his enquiry. *''ehyeh 'asher 'ehyeh'* is his reply. We cannot even be sure how to translate it! Encouraged first by the Septuagint, the ancient Greek translation of the Old Testament, written in the third century BCE, and even more strongly by Jerome's Latin Vulgate of the fourth century CE, most translators of 3.14 and commentators upon it have until recently opted for, 'I am who I am.' That is, admittedly, a possible translation. Those who have adopted it have often understood it as a reply of great profundity, getting us as near as any words can to the heart of the divine essence. But defining the divine essence is not something the theologians of the Old Testament are interested in, or rather they wisely leave it aside as something that cannot be done. We have to remind ourselves we are dealing with story-telling, not philosophy of religion. The Septuagint has, *ego eimi ho on*, 'I am the One Who Is'. Not only does that destroy the symmetry of the Hebrew, it fails to recognize the kind of literature it is dealing with. It turns the drama of storytelling into the argument of philosophy. It will not do, whatever its influence upon Christian doctrine, and upon the great 'I am' sayings of John's Gospel. The Vulgate's *sum qui sum*, 'I am who I am', restores the symmetry and the tautology, but fails to take notice of the rest of the passage to which 3.14 belongs.

If we put God's answer back into the context of this story of his encounter with Moses, then we notice the recurrent phrase 'I will be there', and we notice also what a key role it plays in God's reassurances.[10] Whatever the makers of doctrine might traditionally have preferred, the *story* undoubtedly encourages us to keep the future tense in 3.14. Some translate, 'I will be what I will be'.[11] Everett Fox, following Buber and Rosenzweig's much earlier translation, has, 'I will be-there howsoever I will be-there,'[12] and my own translation, 'I will be there as I will be there', is very close to that.

God is playing with words here, or rather with a single word. The sacred divine name in the Hebrew is, as we know, YHWH. The word behind 'I will be there' is, as we have seen, *'ehyeh*.

God is playing with Moses, also. 'I will be there as I will be there' is not a name. God here is *refusing* to give Moses his name, just as he refused to give it to Jacob at the Jabbok. Hagar might have named the Unnameable One, but that makes no difference: God remains unnameable. All encounters with him remind us of that. 'Tell them I-will-be-there has sent you,' he says. As Robert Carroll says, 'It is playful rather than serious linguistics.'[13]

But it is not nonsense.[14] It encapsulates the reassurance which all God's speeches at the Burning Bush are so concerned to convey: God will not leave his people to their anguish and to any brutal extinction. He will be there. He *will be there*. He will teach Pharaoh a thing or two! For that tyrant and his minions 'I-will-be-there' foretells the demand that they cease their brutality, and hints of a threat of grave consequences if they do not. But for Moses and his people it speaks of the fulfilment of ancient promises and obligations. It speaks of *rescue*. God will bring his people into freedom and give them a fine land of their own, as he promised to Abraham, Isaac and Jacob.

I-will-be-there. In this story, not just the story of this particular passage, but the whole tale of the Exodus from Egypt, that is what God's name means. He slips the name itself into the very next verse of his speech! 'Tell the children of Israel, "*YHWH* ... has sent me to you."' (3.15) Just when Moses is not expecting it! So it was at the Jabbok. Jacob asked for a blessing, seemed to be refused, then was granted one all of a sudden and out of the blue. So it is with God. The reality of his blessings and his wisdom always comes as a surprise. It is never quite what we expected or asked. The one talking with Moses behind the desert may be the Unnameable One, but he will give him his name anyway! Such is the essential paradox of encounter with God, the one who cannot be encountered, and yet chooses to meet with us.

Thus the story explains the name. By itself 'YHWH' is clouded in mystery. But his rescuing his people from Egypt reveals his identity.

God continued and said to Moses, 'Tell the children of Israel, "YHWH, the God of your fathers, the God of Abraham, the God of Isaac, the God of Jacob, has sent me to you." This is my name for ever, this the way I will be remembered from generation to generation. Go, gather the elders of Israel, and tell them, "YHWH, the God of your fathers has appeared to me, the God of Abraham, of Isaac and Jacob, saying, 'I have heeded, oh yes, I have heeded you, and what is being done to you in Egypt! I am resolved that I will bring you up out of the misery of Egypt, to the land of the Canaanite, the Hittite, the Amorite, the Perizzite, the Hivvite and the Jebusite, to a land flowing with milk and honey.'" They will listen to your voice, and you and the elders of Israel will go to the king of Egypt, and will say to him, "YHWH, the God of the Hebrews, has met with us. So now, pray let us go a three days' journey into the desert to sacrifice to YHWH, our God." As for me, I know well that the king of Egypt will not give you leave to go, unless he is handled with a firm hand. So I will put forth my hand and I will strike Egypt with all the extraordinary acts of mine which I am about to perform in its midst. After *that* he will put you forth! And I will give the people favour in the eyes of Egypt, and when you go, you will not go empty-handed. Every woman will ask her neighbour and any woman staying in her house for objects of silver and objects of gold and clothing, and you will put them on your sons and on your daughters. So you will plunder Egypt.' (3.15–22)

Now Moses and we, also, know the God we are dealing with: one who has a sharp ear for the sounds of human suffering; who understands and loathes tyranny; who is aware of his obligations and is determined to fulfil them; who is able to rescue; who dreams of giving freedom and plenty and well-being, and is able to make those dreams a reality, so long as those for whom the vision is held cooperate with him. He is a God on the side of the weak and the oppressed, and against those who use great power to break and to kill. Understandably, the story of the Exodus and the entry into the Promised Land has been a powerful source of hope to oppressed peoples in many parts of the world. Understandably also, many Christian Palestinians in the Holy Land cannot bear it, for they know too well how some Israeli Jews use it to claim the whole land for themselves, and drive their Palestinian neighbours out of their villages and uproot their olive groves. Yet, when they look again, as some of them do, at how God is portrayed in the story of the Exodus, they too find as much hope here as do some of the poor of the Third World.

But Moses, standing there with his sandals removed and shaking still with fear, is not yet in a mood for liberation theology. The 'sign' that God has promised him, that he and the Israelites will serve God at Horeb/Sinai, is of little use to him. It *is* a sign, if you have already read to the end of the story, or at least as far as Exodus 19, but Moses is still in chapters 3 and 4. He cannot see it going down very well with the Israelites, and it will certainly cut no ice with Pharaoh. The demand that the Israelites be allowed to go on a three-day pilgrimage to the mountain sounds specious even to us. Pharaoh will see straight through it. Does not God say so? He tells Moses in so many words that Pharaoh will not take any notice of him. He speaks darkly of 'extraordinary acts' with which he will strike Egypt. That does not make Egypt sound a very safe place to be in. Moses would much rather stay in Midian, minding his father-in-law's sheep and goats. For the third time he protests:

> But Moses answered and said, 'Look, they will not believe me. They will not listen to my voice. No, but they will say, "YHWH did not appear to you." '
> YHWH said to him, 'What is that in your hand?'
> He said, 'A staff.'
> He said, 'Throw it on the ground.'
> He threw it on the ground, and it turned into a snake! Moses ran away from it.
> YHWH said to Moses, 'Put forth your hand and seize it by its tail!'
> He put forth his hand and grasped it, and it turned into a staff in his grip.
> 'That's so they will believe that YHWH did appear to you,

the God of their ancestors, the God of Abraham, the God of Isaac, the God of Jacob.' (4.1–5)

Again YHWH said to him, 'Put your hand inside your cloak.'

He put his hand inside his cloak. When he took it out, see, his hand was leprous, like snow!

He said, 'Put your hand back inside your cloak.'

He put his hand back inside his cloak. When he took it out from his cloak, see, it was back to normal, just like the rest of his skin!

'Now if they do not believe you, nor listen to the voice of the first sign, they will believe the voice of the second one. If they still do not believe these two signs, and do not listen to your voice, then you shall take some water from the Nile and pour it on the dry ground. And the water you take from the Nile will become blood on the dry ground. (6–9)

These signs are not primarily for Moses' benefit. At least, that is not how they are presented. God clearly means to give him the power to perform them himself in front of the Israelites back in Egypt, to convince *them*. In fact, the narrative will go on to tell of the first being performed by Aaron, Moses' brother, in front of Pharaoh and his courtiers (7.8–13), and the third will become the first of the plagues of Egypt, with the whole of the Nile being turned to blood (7.14–24; the second sign will not be repeated). Both of them will signal the triumph of God, and the destruction of the gods of Egypt. For the scene of Pharaoh's court will be set in the vicinity of the Delta region, and the king will be wearing on the front of his crown the head of the snake-goddess, Wadjet, to signify his divine authority over that northern part of his kingdom. His magicians also will produce snakes out of their staffs of office, but their snakes will be promptly gobbled up by Aaron's. So much for Wadjet! So much for Pharaoh and all his works! The Nile also was worshipped by the Egyptians as the god Hapi, and the god will be beaten by Aaron (the verb used in the Hebrew of 7.20, and in the prior command of 7.17, is the same as the one employed in 2.11 of the Egyptian beating the Hebrew slave), till his blood runs wide and he dies and begins to decompose. On the surface

13

the events will seem like acts in a grim pantomime. Beneath their surface, however, a titanic contest will be being fought between the God of an insignificant slave people, and the gods and the king of an ancient Near Eastern superpower.

For the moment Moses is lost for words, but not in the way God would wish. Moses is not ready for Wagner, any more than he is for liberation theology. For him the signs *are* mere pantomime, an empty display of magic. He is being asked to confront an Adolf Hitler, not a Paul Daniels. He tries again, for the fourth time:

> But Moses said to YHWH, 'Excuse me, my lord, I am no man of words. Not me. Not yesterday. Not the day before that. Not since you have spoken to your servant, either. For I am slow-and-heavy of mouth, and slow-and-heavy of tongue, I am.'
>
> YHWH said to him, 'Who has given speech to human beings, or who is it who makes them mute or deaf, sighted or blind? Is it not I, YHWH? So now, go. I myself will be there with your mouth, and will teach you what to say.' (4.10–12)

Some have understood Moses to mean he has a physical handicap, a severe stammer, perhaps, when he is nervous, or dysphasia, an inability to get the words out he wishes to speak. More likely, his objection is a mere pretext, another sign of his fear of the task confronting him, and another attempt to wriggle out of it, and, for God, another chance to give reassurance.[15] Certainly we have seen no speech defect in Moses as yet. If there has been one, then God cures it here, by promising to 'be there with [his] mouth'. The Moses we will encounter in the subsequent narrative will not be short on eloquence or fluency. God makes a concession to him in his final speech in this episode of the Burning Bush, and allows him to take his brother Aaron along with him back to Egypt, as his spokesman. That concession, however, is more artificial than real. It is given, not because any handicap of Moses' makes it necessary, but because by that stage in the dialogue God is at the end of his tether, and cannot take further argument. When it comes to it, the part Aaron plays in Egypt will be very small, and only once will we be told he does the speaking for his younger brother (4.30).

Yet we know, and Moses knows, that back in Egypt it will not be just a matter of words. The greatest eloquence will not be enough, and will probably count for nothing. Three times now God has given him his marching orders, and told him to go. Three times has a sense of completeness and finality about it. Yet in desperation Moses tries once more, and comes as near as he dare to refusing to go:

> But he said, 'Excuse me, my lord, please send someone else, anyone else you care to send!'
>
> YHWH's anger flared up against Moses, and he said, 'Is there not Aaron, your brother, the Levite? He will speak. *He* will speak. I know that. Look, he is coming out to meet you, and when he sees you, his heart will be glad. Speak to him and put the words in his mouth, and I myself will be there with your mouth and with his mouth, and I will teach you both what to do. He will be the one to speak on your behalf to the people, and he, he will be your mouth, while you will be his god. Take this staff in your hand. You will use it to perform the signs.' (4.13–17)

With that the scene comes to an abrupt end. God goes on his way, and Moses returns to Jethro, his father-in-law, to get permission to go back to Egypt.

At the end of this episode, still facing the Burning Bush, Moses has suddenly found it blazing with God's anger against *him*. God has finally lost all patience with him, and will brook no further protest. There is a job to be done, and Moses must play his part in it. That is vital, and that is all there is to it. Indeed, it would seem that Moses has been dealing with a *fait accompli* all along. Aaron, of whom we have heard nothing before this moment, is already on his way to meet his brother! God has had it all sewn up from the start! There has been no real discussion, no movement in the mind of God, as there was for a time above the plain of Sodom in Genesis 18, when he was taught a lesson in justice and holiness by Abraham.[16] God is not yet speaking to Moses face to face *as one speaks to a friend*. There is as yet no mutuality about their relationship. That is still to come. Moses must accept his orders, and in the end must go without argument.

Yet this remarkable dialogue, remarkable in Old Testament terms for its sheer length for a start, does change things. Moses' protests allow God to begin to get near him. This man is no automaton, nor an obsequious slave. He may dissemble in this passage, and save his candour with God for a later time, but he does not retreat behind the walls of polite piety. He is at points in the dialogue deferential, but deference does not determine the nature of the relationship. It is only God's determination to see justice done in Egypt that does that. God has found a person at Horeb with whom he will be able to do business.

As a token of that he transforms Moses' shepherd's crook into a staff of divine office, filled to its tip with the power to work wonders. It will be called 'the staff of God' (4.20). Moses has been using it to tap sheep's or goats' backsides. One day he will use it to part the waters of the Red Sea.

God has found someone here with whom one day he *will* be able to speak as one speaks to a friend. Sooner than perhaps he cares for, he will hear Moses speak with a new, more powerful voice. It will contain no dissembling at all, but will be full of an anger to match any fury of his own.

Moses has only begun with God. God has only begun with Moses.

2

Plain Speaking

(Exodus 5.22–3; Numbers 11.10–15)

At the Burning Bush dialogue is initiated by God, and closed by God. He calls to Moses out of the bush and commands his attention. He decides when he has had enough of Moses' protestations, and brings the meeting to its sudden ending. His authority is clear and cannot be gainsaid. Once Moses is back in Egypt, however, a different song is sung.

Its tones suit the brutality of the place. This Egypt is not the Egypt we ourselves know from its glittering trail of artefacts. It is not the brilliant civilization now so admired for its cultural and scientific achievements, and for its relative stability over three millennia. Nor is it the sophisticated society we glimpse in the Joseph story of Genesis. No longer is it a society where a foreigner like Joseph can rise to dizzy heights of power, where an imprisoned slave can become the second most powerful person in the land by claiming to read the mind of God. True, the Pharaoh of the attempted holocaust of Exodus 1 is dead, but his successor is little better. He does not attempt genocide, yet the Israelites are still subject to that same forced labour with which the first Pharaoh began his oppression. Dark paranoia and obstinate cruelty still walk the corridors of power. Moses is in a country where his people are under the lash, where heads are bowed and backs near breaking, where shouted orders and cries of agony punctuate a terrible silence, and bodies lie crumpled in the sand.

When Moses and his brother Aaron first approach Pharaoh to demand an end to it all, they only make things worse. They carry with them those words of God that will ring out down the centuries, wherever one people is oppressed by another: 'Let my people go!'. 'Who is the Lord that I should heed his voice and let Israel go?' is the Pharaoh's immediate response

(Exodus 5.1–2). This is his first speech in the text, and it demonstrates both his insight and his ignorance. On the one hand he sees the authority of this unknown god as an immediate challenge to his own, which of course it is. Never, in fact, will he come to terms with it. On the other hand he does not recognize who he is up against. All he sees is two troublemakers, a slave people needing urgently to be taught a lesson, and an opportunity to give the screw of oppression another vicious turn. He is a bully and understands his trade. Once Moses and Aaron have gone, he issues new orders to the slave-drivers: the Israelites are to continue to produce the same number of bricks, but now they are to gather the straw to make them, instead of having it provided for them.

The new conditions are meant to be intolerable, and so they are. The people find it impossible to meet their daily quotas, and their own supervisors are beaten for their failure. They complain to Pharaoh, but as we might have anticipated, they are quickly sent packing. All they take away with them is an accusation that the Israelites are lazy, and a reiteration of the orders. Moses and Aaron are waiting outside the palace to meet them. 'May the Lord look upon you and judge!' they cry. 'You have made our smell stink before Pharaoh and his officials! You have put a sword into their hands, to slaughter us!' (5.21) Aaron says nothing. Till the story of the Golden Calf he remains a shadowy figure, who never speaks for himself. Not so Moses! Not so Moses! Moses turns to the only one he can turn to. He addresses God.

> 'My lord, why have you brought disaster to this people? Why the hell did you send me? Ever since I came to Pharaoh to speak in your name, he has brought disaster to this people! And as for rescuing, you have not rescued your people!' (5.22–3)

Moses' speech mirrors in both its tone and its content the words of the supervisors to him and his brother. It gives vent to their anger as well as his own. It cries their pain also, their frustration, their terror, their powerlessness. Yet Moses does not stand on the sidelines of their suffering. He also is on the pitch, and plays Pharaoh's brutal game to Pharaoh's bitter rules. He does not only pray on behalf of others. In the few lines of his prayer he bares his own soul before God and shows him its dark recesses. 'Why the hell did you send me?' He too is suffering. He looks his God straight in the eye and tells him so.

We have not heard God addressed like this in the Bible before. In the Garden of Eden the man made the sly accusation, 'That woman you gave to be with me, she gave me fruit from the tree and I ate' (Genesis 3.12). In the next chapter of Genesis, Cain loudly protested that his guilt or wickedness or punishment was too great for him to bear (4.13–14). Later, most astonishingly, Abraham told God he would effectively cease to be God if he were to destroy the good people of Sodom along with the bad (18.23–5).[1] But this God in Egypt is under verbal attack. Moses' words are savage with anger. He makes a direct comparison between God and Pharaoh, and a devastating one it is: they have both brought nothing but disaster to his people; God also is the enemy; he is another thug, and the Israelites are victims of his brutality also. Only Job will take the prayer of lament and complaint further than this.

Moses' second question, 'Why the hell did you send me?' reminds us of his protests at the Burning Bush, but only superficially. Here is no clinging onto security and the family comforts of Midian. Moses is in the furnace of Egypt now, and there seems no way out. Here is no attempt to escape, but a demand for a plain answer. Here is no making of excuses, but the integrity of serious accusation. He does not hide his face from God any more, but shakes his fist at him. This time no trying to wriggle out of what he has to do, but the fearless stating of harsh reality, as he sees and feels it.

We may wish to question his theology. We may wish to reassure him that God is never a thug, and tell him that the notion of God's hostility is absurd. But perhaps we are quick to correct him because we ourselves are not in his Egypt. In the calm and security of our Midian, if that is where we are, we do not feel for a moment that God is against us, and we find such a thought inconceivable. Those, however, who live with brutal political regimes and struggle to survive, or many who have been struck by personal tragedy, will at once recognize the 'truth' of Moses' words. Their world is dominated by dark powers that batter them to pieces. Either God is excluded altogether, or else he must be attacking them himself. That is what it *feels* like, whatever the theologians (who, in their denial of God's enmity, are right, of course) may say. Moses' prayer does not stem from careful theological debate, but from the white heat of human experience at its most bewildering and its most painful.

Yet his words undermine themselves. They accuse God of being a thug, but people do not speak to thugs like that. With thugs people keep silent, or are carefully sycophantic, or else hide themselves, if they can, in the entourage of someone more powerful. Moses may compare God to a vicious Pharaoh, but his own speeches to that same Pharaoh in these chapters of Exodus are more polite, or else they are prefaced by 'Thus says YHWH', and so declare themselves as having a higher and impregnable authority. Moses' prayer to God, by contrast, uses the language of the lover to the beloved, the language of the blazing row, employed by those who feel they have been grievously let down. It is the talk of those who expect help, who expect loyalty, reliability, protection from the one to whom they speak, for that is what they have experienced in the past. Such prayer as this does not stem from a conviction that God is essentially cruel. On the contrary, it betrays the belief that he is invariably merciful and compassionate. Moses prays as he does on the understanding that God has a sharp eye for oppression and an acute ear for pain. Did he not tell him at the Burning Bush that he had seen the misery of the Israelites and heard their cries of anguish? Moses prays like this because he believes that God is under obligation to rescue his people when they need him. Did he not promise at Horeb to do just that? Moses prays like this because God seems to be acting out of character, because nothing makes sense, because faith and truth seem to be betrayed.

But if this is indeed the language of the row between lovers or close friends, then God does not respond in kind. No 'How dare you compare me to that monster of a Pharaoh?!', but instead a calm assurance that he will use all his powers to rescue his people and bring them into freedom (6.1–8). Nowhere in the Old Testament is prayer like this condemned, even when it is as forceful, as shocking in its accusations, as this one of Moses. He prays with passion and integrity, and that is enough. He demands God's attention, calls upon his ancient intimacy, and he receives them. He means to stir him into action, and most certainly he succeeds. His prayer stems from the conviction that God can and will act. He will not be disappointed. The stories of the following chapters will be those of the plagues and the crossing of the Red Sea.

Only twice, in the rare security of a theological college chapel, have I heard prayer like this in the context of Christian worship. We Christians have forgotten how to pray like this. Many of us have been carefully taught not to pray like this.

* * *

It is not the only example of its kind in the Moses stories. There is another in Numbers 11. This one comes late in the story of the Israelites living in the desert between Egypt and the Promised Land. The people are not bedouin. The desert is not their home, and they do not have the resources to make it so. Before they came to discover its own peculiar deprivations they knew nothing but slavery. In Egypt they could not order life for themselves, and in the desert they are quite incapable of doing so. The crossing of the Red Sea, for all its wonder, has hardly provided them with the skills for independent living. They are like helpless children, and that is precisely how they behave.

The long story of their life in the desert includes their receiving the Torah at Sinai/Horeb. God gives his people what is in effect the fruit of the Tree of the Knowing of Good and Evil. No longer is it forbidden, as it was in the Garden. The people are grown up now, or rather they need to achieve maturity before they enter the Land and establish themselves as a nation. Nor do they have to stretch up to take the fruit as the woman did, for Moses comes down the mountain with baskets full. And yet this story of the wilderness, that should be so full of triumphant joy, becomes a sorry tale of rebelliousness, divine anger and punishment.[2]

By the time the people reach Numbers 11 they have been eating manna for a long time. This strange food that seems to come from heaven, and which has enabled them to survive in

21

their barren surroundings for so many years, has more than begun to pall. They long for meat and vegetables. The manna has ceased to be a sign to them of God's generosity, and instead has become a symbol of their plight, stuck as they are in a hostile desert, between Egypt and a Promised Land that still seems so remote. The people stand weeping at the entrances to their tents. Moses flies into a rage.

His anger seems excessive, until we recall the previous occasions on which the people have provoked him. In the book of Exodus scarcely are they across the Red Sea, when they begin to complain about the lack of food and water. With an absurd nostalgia they imagine the period in Egypt was a golden age, dreaming that they sat round the flesh pots and ate their fill. They blame Moses and Aaron for their plight and accuse them of bringing them into the desert to kill them (Exodus 15.22–17.7). That is bad enough, but much worse is to come. While Moses is speaking with God on the summit of Sinai, and receiving yet more of the secrets of the divine heart to take down to the people, they decide they can wait for him no longer, and make a new god, contained in a calf of gold, for their worship and their gratitude (Exodus 32.1–6). This tragic episode we will be considering in more detail in our next two chapters, but it needs to be borne in mind as we turn to Numbers 11, for it helps to explain the size of Moses' anger.

So does his exhaustion. Back in Exodus 18 his father-in-law, Jethro, warns him that he will soon be worn out if he continues to bear the burden of leadership and decide all legal matters for the people on his own. Jethro recommends that he set up a judicial system which will allow him to delegate most of the work to others, and he at once acts upon that advice. Yet we do not hear a great deal of these other officials in the narrative, and, of course, the episode of the Golden Calf is enough to demonstrate how much the people still depend on Moses' leadership, if they are to remain recognizably the people of the God who brought them out of Egypt and gave them the fruits of his wisdom.

Numbers 11 further reveals to us the nature and persistence of that dependence. Moses is still on his own. At least, that is the reality of it as far as he is concerned. He is near the end of his tether, and when the people start complaining about the manna, and bring up again their ridiculously romantic reminiscences about an Egypt that never was, something in him snaps. But not before God himself gets angry. For Moses that anger might appear to make things worse and provide his breaking-point.

> Moses heard the people weeping in their clans, each man at the entrance of his tent. The anger of YHWH exploded, and it was ill in Moses' eyes. (Numbers 11.10)

What, we might ask, does that 'it' refer to? Is it to the people's crying, or to God's anger? The Hebrew is ambiguous, and Moses' prayer that follows lets the uncertainty remain. We are free to decide for ourselves.

> Moses said to YHWH, 'Why have you brought disaster upon your servant? Why have I not found grace in your eyes? To put the burden of this entire people upon me! Am *I* the one who conceived this entire people? Am *I* the one who gave them birth, that you should say to me, "Carry them in your arms, as a nursing mother carries her suckling child," until they reach the land you promised on oath to their ancestors? Where shall I find meat to give this entire people? For they weep all over me, saying, "Give us meat that we may eat!" I cannot carry this entire people all by myself. They are too heavy for me! If that is the way you are going to treat me, then pray kill me, yes, kill me, if I have found any grace in your eyes, that I may not look upon my disaster.' (11.11–15)

As in Exodus 5, his prayer starts with 'Why?', and a second 'Why?' soon follows. The prayers of lament and complaint that are so prominent in the Old Testament can be described as variations on the theme of that question: 'Why? *Why?*' This kind of prayer does not give up easily. This kind of prayer does not give up at all! It demands an answer, and continues till it gets one. Job, in his own agony and bewilderment, will persist for some sixteen chapters!

The opening phrase is the same as the one in Exodus 5: 'Why have you brought disaster upon . . .' This second prayer both opens and closes with 'disaster'. That is its theme from beginning to end. This time, however, for reasons we have already tried to explain, Moses is primarily concerned about himself. Even when he refers to the people's desire for meat, he concentrates upon his own inability to provide it, and the effect of their incessant demands upon him.

The stress and the loneliness of his office is clear, and all those who bear great responsibilities, especially within hierarchical organizations, will recognize the plausibility of the language here. Over the years his position, as well as his persistent loyalty to God, have put him at a distance from the rest of the people, and here, as Norman Whybray points out,[3] he distances himself further. Four times he calls them not 'my people', or 'your [meaning God's] people', but 'this people', as if he himself does not belong to them. With unwitting irony, he speaks of *them* reaching the Promised Land, as if he himself will not be among them. (Little does he know at this juncture, that he will indeed die the wrong side of the Jordan.)

At the same time the dominant image he employs underlines the closeness of his involvement with the people. He has been acting as their 'mother', carrying them upon his hip, listening to their clamour for food. With devastating simplicity, and with tight-lipped humour, he cries, 'They are too heavy for me!' '*You*, God,' he says in effect, 'are their mother. *You* were the one who conceived them, who carried them in the womb, who gave them birth. They are *your* responsibility. They are *yours*, not mine, to look after.' Prayers of complaint against God in the Old Testament frequently accuse God of not fulfilling his obligations, as this one does. Moses' prayer in Exodus 5 did so, and with similar force and clarity.

Within the Christian or Jewish traditions the image of the mother is still not commonly used of God, and it is relatively scarce in the Old Testament. In our final chapter we will come across it in Job, and it is present also in Genesis 49.25 ('by God Almighty, may he bless you ... with blessings of the breasts and of the womb!'); Deuteronomy 32.18 ('The Rock that gave you birth, you neglected; you forgot the God who writhed in labour with you'); in the beautiful poem of Hosea 11.1–9 ('it was I who nursed Ephraim, taking him in my arms ... And I was for them like those who take a nursling to the breast, and I bowed down to him to give him suck'[4]); in Isaiah 42.14 ('now

24

I will cry out like a woman in labour, gasp and pant'); 46.3 ('Listen to me, house of Jacob, . . . who have been borne by me from birth, carried from the womb'); 49.15 ('Can a woman forget her nursing child, or show no compassion for the child of her womb? Even these may forget, but I will not forget you'); 66.13 ('As a child whom his mother comforts, so I will comfort you').[5] More powerfully than the metaphor or title of 'father', 'mother' evokes a sense of God's intimacy and compassion. And that is why Moses uses it here. For intimacy and compassion are precisely what he feels God has denied him. He, or rather she, has deserted him, left him to carry the people all on his own, with no thought for what that is doing to him.

His prayer ends dramatically with an invitation to God to kill him. We are reminded of Elijah at Horeb in 1 Kings 19.4, or Jonah in Jonah 4.3. All three ask God to kill them because they find the tasks assigned to them by God unbearable. All three, and Moses most especially, can command our sympathy. All three are refused their request, and told, one way or another, to get on with the job. God tells Elijah in effect to stop being so melodramatic, and Jonah is challenged by curious pantomime, then by a devastating question, to come to terms with the divine mercy and forgiveness that has driven him to such distraction. Moses also has much still to do.

Yet in his case God recognizes the validity of his grievances, and promises practical help. He assures him that he will give seventy of the elders of the people a share of the spirit he has given to Moses himself, so that they can take some of the load of leadership from off his shoulders. He tells him, also, that he will provide meat for the people. Boldly Moses questions his ability to do that: 'Six hundred thousand on foot are the people that I am with, and you, you say "I will give them meat and they will eat for an entire month"! Are there flocks and herds to be slaughtered for them, to give them enough? If all the fish in the sea were caught for them, would that give them enough?' (11.21–2) His words remind us of the bewilderment of Jesus' disciples when faced with feeding five or four thousand people in open country, but Moses' questioning is much more forceful, and casts more obvious doubt upon the powers of the divine. He is still at the end of his tether. His anger and frustration, his sense that God has let him down, still fill his speech. In reply God reassures him of his ability to provide all that the people need.

For us, however, God's reassurances turn out to be most *un*reassuring. He engineers a wreck of quails of supernatural and quite ridiculous proportions, and then gives the people a sinister craving to collect and eat the birds until the meat is coming out of their nostrils and they die in huge numbers from the surfeit. Gift turns out to be fearful punishment. There is no generosity in it at all, only a terrifying abuse of divine power.[6] Furthermore, as Whybray has pointed out,[7] God only acts after Moses has drawn his attention to the problems, as if he has not appreciated them before, or not cared.

Undoubtedly, the theology is flawed here, and grievously so. There is more to be said, however, than just that. The Old Testament writers show great boldness in depicting the effect upon God of his relations with us human beings. We can drive him to such grief, that he determines to wipe out almost his entire creation. We can show him how to act as judge of the whole earth, and shift his focus, at least for a spell. Moses moves God's mind here, and by the terms of Old Testament theology we should not be too surprised about that. Furthermore, the movement within God indicates again his intimacy with Moses. Though Moses calls himself God's 'servant', and later in his prayer, with bitter sarcasm, bends and touches his forelock to him – 'if I have found any grace in your eyes' – yet he still speaks as the lover to the beloved, as he did in Exodus 5, even if here the relationship is showing greater strain. As Whybray remarks with amazement, he 'addresses God, as it were, on a basis of equality'.[8] The text of Exodus puts it more poetically:

YHWH would speak to Moses face to face, as one speaks to a friend. (33.11)

With those few words of marvellous simplicity, the narrator sums up the relationship that God and Moses enjoy, at least from Exodus 5.22–3 onwards. We remarked towards the end of our discussion of the Burning Bush that as yet there was no mutuality about their relationship. From 5.22–3, where Moses hurls such bitter pain in God's face, there is. It is as if such plain speaking *creates* the intimacy.

Should we be surprised by that? Not at all. And should we be surprised that the much more cautious, much more polite, much less candid language of the generality of Christian public prayer succeeds in keeping God at arm's length? Not at all. It is designed to do just that. We Christians, who speak so quickly and so insistently of the love of God, have much to learn about God and about prayer from this Moses.

3

Another Go-between

(Exodus 32.7–14; Numbers 14.11–25; Exodus 32.30–5)

In that prayer of his in Exodus 5.22–3 that we discussed in our last chapter Moses does not only pray on others' behalf. He cries his own pain, also. Yet he *does*, of course, pray for others. The supervisors of the people, who have just had such a rough ride from Pharaoh, do not turn to God themselves, but to Moses and his brother. Earlier in the story, when first the sound of the anguish of the people reaches heaven, the narrator does not describe them as praying to God, only as crying out in their distress (Exodus 2.23). As Job will do at first, they cry into the dark and hurl their pain into the void. God hears them, not because they address him, but because he has a keen ear for their suffering.

So it will remain in these stories of Moses. He will be the go-between. The people will not approach God themselves. For the most part they will not be able to. Sinai, the mountain on which God descends, becomes so charged with his holiness that they are forbidden to touch it on pain of death (Exodus 19.12–13). They will remain but bystanders to theophany, to this momentous appearing of God on earth. Except for one occasion, God's intimacy will be reserved for Moses alone. At one point God invites his brother Aaron to approach him, together with two of his sons, Nadab and Abihu, and seventy of the elders (Exodus 24.1), and the text boldly goes on to describe all this number seeing God, and sitting and eating in his presence. With singular audacity it begins to describe their vision: 'They saw the God of Israel, and beneath his feet something like tiles of sapphire, something like the substance of heaven for clarity' (24.10). But the narrative quickly reverts to the usual talk of Moses going up to God, admittedly with his assistant Joshua, to receive the tablets bearing the Torah, and once again the others are left behind (24.12–14). As far as the rest of the people are concerned, the God of Sinai will remain hidden in a dense mist surrounding the summit, and they can only look on as Moses disappears into it (20.21). The nearest they will get to a vision of God will be the sight of his glory burning on the mountain like a consuming fire (24.17). When Moses comes down from the mountain and pitches his Tent of Meeting, still they will have to be content to stand at the entrance to their own tents and watch as Moses, with Joshua, enters the divine presence (33.7–11).

Joshua will remain for the time being a shadowy figure, present as only an occasional mention in the text. Though his position as Moses' assistant can bring him very close to God, his own dealings with God are not touched upon, and will not be so till Moses is dead. Only Moses will speak to God face to face, as one speaks to a friend. In a rare moment the writer of Deuteronomy will tell us that YHWH spoke 'face to face' with the whole people, when he gave them the Ten Commandments, but in the very next verse he seems to correct himself by having Moses say he was standing between God and the people at the time (Deuteronomy 5.4–5). After the Ten Commandments only Moses will hear what God is saying, and even with those first commandments the people are so terrified by the sound of God's voice, that they retreat to a safe distance and beg Moses to approach God on their behalf (Exodus 20.18–21; and the more elaborate version in Deuteronomy 5.22–7). At that point the sound of God's speaking is audible to the people (19.9), as the sound of his footsteps was to the couple in the Garden of Eden, but even then it is not entirely clear how much they can make out for themselves. God's words seem to be nearly drowned out by thunder and the insistent call of the ram's horn (Exodus 19.16, 19; 20.18), while in the parallel account in Deuteronomy Moses still has to act as interpreter (5.5). The people need him to turn the sounds of heaven into intelligible earthly speech. They depend on him to turn the terrifying cacophony of Sinai into the wisdom of Torah.

Such is God's intimacy with Moses, that he comes down the mountain from the divine presence with his face shining with its glory. Sinai is not Moses' Mount of Transfiguration, for that glory is not his own, but is borrowed from the God he meets there. Yet the light is so bright, so awesome, that those who see him are afraid to come near him, and he has to cover himself with a veil (34.29–35).

We, the hearers and the readers of the story, are allowed by the narrator to accompany Moses and hear what God has to say to him. It is a rare privilege, indeed, but even we cannot see what Moses sees. The mention of the mist, the fire, or the sapphire pavement beneath God's feet, is the nearest the narrator will bring us to seeing what Moses sees. For us also Moses disappears into that strange mist, or through the flaps of the Tent of Meeting. (Even for Moses large mystery will remain, as we will discover in our next chapter.) Though we hear so very many words at Sinai, the greater part of the truth will remain hidden, as of course it must, for God is essentially a mystery, and those who pretend otherwise are always talking about something else. There is an unassailable privacy about Moses' encounters with God, and a sense in which they are his very exclusive privilege.

Have we got another Joseph here? Joseph is also a go-between. Everyone else in Joseph's family or Joseph's Egypt relies on him to reveal the mind of God, as the Israelites later come to rely on Moses. The beginnings of their stories also contain what might seem a significant parallel. When Joseph first comes on the scene, brandishing his dream of his family's sheaves of corn bowing down to his own, his brothers protest with, 'King! Will you play king over us? Rule! Will you rule over us?' (Genesis 37.8) When Moses emerges from Pharaoh's palace where he has been brought up, and attempts to intervene in a quarrel between two of his own people, one of them turns on him and says, 'Who set you up as a prince and judge over us?' (Exodus 2.14) Both story and history seem to be repeating themselves here.

As we proceed further into the narratives, however, obvious and large differences between Moses and Joseph soon emerge. From beginning to end Joseph is supremely confident of his wisdom. Moses, on the other hand, protests five times to God at the Burning Bush that he is not the man for the job being given him, and when, much later, he comes down from Sinai with his face blazing with the glory of God, he is not aware of it (Exodus

34.29). While Joseph's interpretations of dreams, both his own and those of others, all turn out to be correct, we can question his understanding of the ways of God. The teaching Moses conveys to the people in the desert, however, is unequivocally presented as the wisdom of God himself. 'God spoke all these words, saying ...', is how the Ten Words, or Ten Commandments, are introduced (20.1), and after that further collections of teaching are prefaced with words such as, 'YHWH spoke to Moses, saying, "Speak to the children of Israel ..."' (25.1–2a). We are also told, 'Moses came and recounted to the people all the words of YHWH and all the regulations' (24.3), and that the stone tablets of the covenant were not only given to him by God, but were written by God's finger (31.18). The narrator seeks to leave us in no doubt. At every turn he assures us that the Torah is not composed by Moses, but is God's work and represents God's mind. Moses is merely the messenger boy. 'Joseph is an expert. But is he always *right*?' we asked in our book, *Looking God in the Eye*.[1] Genesis allowed, even encouraged us to ask that. Exodus and the subsequent books of the Torah make it quite impossible to ask such a question of Moses. If we doubt the truth of the Torah or of some particular provisions of it, then we have to take our unease to the God of these books, or to those anonymous teachers of ancient Israel who compiled the material and handed it down to us. Joseph 'is too full of his expertise', we wrote in *Looking God in the Eye*. 'He gets in the way. Putting his opulent figure between us and God, he hides him from us and obscures his purposes.'[2] We could not conceivably make such a statement about Moses. He tells his people, and conveys to us, the hearers and readers of his story, as much as he can, and puts the declared wisdom of God in our hands. Moses and Joseph are both go-betweens, but they could hardly be more different from one another.

Yet Moses *is* a go-between. This is not the Garden of Eden. His stories lack the subversive egalitarianism of that earlier tale. The summit of Sinai or the Tent of Meeting are not for the likes of you and me. It is no longer enough for us to be human in order to gain access to the holy of holies and speak with God face to face. Now we have to be singled out, called and given a special portion of the spirit of God. We may be told that the tablets were written by the finger of God, but priests, Israelite priests, have left their own fingerprints all over them. Moses is not portrayed as a priest himself, though he ordains his brother Aaron as one, and yet he reminds us inescapably of the most privileged of those who conducted the worship in the temple in Jerusalem, and the power they exercised. His stories challenge the *political* establishment, for they speak so powerfully of the sovereignty of God, and do not allow any human ruler to claim the credit of the Torah for himself. But they do not question the *religious* establishment. Quite the reverse, they make a large claim for its authority. Those of us who belong to that establishment, in whatever form it might be, must beware of pride or complacency as we read these stories!

*   *   *

Lest we be too quick to identify ourselves with Moses and make a bid for his privileges, the narrative reminds us that being a go-between, when one of the parties involved is God, can be an uncomfortable business! It is time to turn, as we promised, to the episode of the Golden Calf.

Moses has been hidden away on the summit of Sinai for a long time, forty days and forty nights, as the text has it (24.18). The people get fed up of waiting. 'We do not know what has happened to him,' they tell Aaron (32.1). But they do not suggest Aaron might climb up himself (as he did in chapter 24, when he went with two of his sons and the seventy elders) to look for him. No. They decide to change gods! They appear not to know what has happened to their God either. 'Make us a god to go before us!' they say to Aaron. 'Make us a god'! As if such a thing is possible! But Aaron seems to think it is perfectly within his capabilities. Out of the gold the people took from the Egyptians before escaping to the Red Sea (Exodus 14.35–6), he makes a calf. The people are delighted, positively overcome! 'This is your god, O Israel,' they cry, 'who brought you up out of the land of Egypt!' (32.4) Aaron declares it is time to have a festival, ambiguously calls it 'a festival to YHWH', and the next day the people offer sacrifices to celebrate their alliance with their new god and to declare their gratitude, and then finish with a rare old party.

In Egypt they saw the things their God could do. They saw what he did at the Red Sea. Since leaving the Sea they have witnessed the miracles of the bitter water at Marah being made sweet, of the provision of the manna, of the rock being split at Massah and Meribah to become a fountain of yet more water. They know what YHWH has done for them. They know that without him they would have died of thirst and starvation. But they have forgotten. They have witnessed his terrifying glory descending upon Sinai. They have heard the awesome tones of the divine voice. Aaron, the god-maker, has even been up Sinai with seventy-two of them, and *seen* God for himself, and that beautiful pavement beneath his feet! But all that, quite inexplicably, seems forgotten too. They have all reverted again to behaving like small children.

Still shrouded by that awesome mist on the summit of the mountain, Moses remains blissfully unaware of what is going on down below. God sees and hears all.

> YHWH spoke to Moses, 'Go, go down! For your people, whom you brought out of Egypt, have ruined everything! They have been quick to turn aside from the way I commanded them. They have made themselves a calf out of molten metal! They have prostrated themselves before it! They have sacrificed to it! They have said, "*This* is your God, Israel, who brought you up out of the land of Egypt!"
>
> And YHWH said to Moses, 'I have seen this people. What a stiff-necked people they are! So now, let me alone, that my anger may flare up against them and I may consume them! Then I can turn *you* into a great nation!' (Exodus 32.7–10)

In the generality of Christian discourse we no longer seem to talk much of the anger of God, unless it is to bolster up some hideous belief in a God who would punish homosexuals with AIDS, or consign Muslims to the fires of hell. Such belief as that is hideous partly because it is so calculating. However much passion may infuse its expression, it so clearly comes from the darkness of human prejudice and fear, and is so full of nervous self-righteousness. This divine anger of Exodus 32 contains fear, but no prejudice or self-righteousness. Nor is it calculated, but wild and extravagant. It is an explosion of divine grief. The people have tried God's patience ever since the crossing of the sea. Now that they have so decisively turned their backs on him, after all he has done for them, after all he has given them, he can take no more. He snaps. He did so on one famous occasion much earlier in this great story. The violence of humanity caused him such pain that he decided to wipe them out, together with the rest of his creation. He chose then to preserve just one family, and start again with Noah.

Noah did not argue with him. He maintained an unnerving silence throughout. But then, Noah and God did not speak with one another face to face. Noah did not speak back at all. There was no dialogue. Noah was not Moses.

> Moses soothed the face of YHWH his God, and said, 'Why, YHWH, should your anger flare up against your people, when you have led them out of the land of Egypt with such great power and such a strong hand? Why should the Egyptians say, "It was for evil he brought them out, to slaughter them in the mountains and wipe them off the face of the earth"? Turn back from the blaze of your anger! Change your mind! Do not bring such disaster upon your people! Remember Abraham, Isaac and Israel, your servants. You swore them an oath, by your own self. You told them, "I will make your descendants as many as the stars of the heavens, and all this land I have promised I will give to your descendants, and they will inherit it for eternity."' (32.11–14)

Sometimes the writers of these narratives manage to contain a whole world in a tiny handful of words. 'Moses soothed the face of YHWH his God' is an example. 'YHWH would speak to Moses face to face, as one speaks to a friend' is another. Both encapsulate the remarkable familiarity of their relationship and its even more remarkable mutuality. This example from the story of the Golden Calf is especially moving, for it expresses such pathos and such human tenderness. Moses does the work we might, in our own storytelling, assign to an angel. We might even prefer to leave it to the members of the Trinity to sort each other out. Moses is never deified in these stories, nor made superhuman. As James Nohrnberg says, 'Before God Moses is always the representative of the human, not the superhuman.'[3] Yet in this clause, in the five or six Hebrew words of 'Moses soothed the face of YHWH his God,' he seems to step inside the circle of the divine. It is perhaps as bold a statement of the intimacy between a human being and God as we will find anywhere in the Old Testament.

But let us not get sentimental! This is no gentle domestic scene. This God is in a rage! Moses has leaped into the white heat of the divine anger to snatch his people out of the flames. It is an act of extraordinary bravery. We see at once how very far Moses has come since all that protesting and dissembling at the Burning Bush.

He tells God that his plan to destroy his people is complete nonsense. Whatever we may think about the part God played in the plague stories and the havoc he wrought, we have to admit that he went to enormous trouble to free his people from slavery. His parting of the Red Sea was comparable to his second act of creation, when he divided the primeval Ocean in two and turned its chaos into a life-giving force.[4] As Moses here implies, it makes no sense to destroy his people now, when he has come thus far with them.

Yet, Moses continues, it is more than a matter of good sense. It is a matter of God's good name. What will the Egyptians think of him? They will conclude that he had no love for his people at all, but was playing a frightful game with them, tantalizing them with promises of rescue, freedom and a land of their own, just so he could take them into the mountains of the desert and annihilate them. The Egyptians will think the God of Israel is another Cain, enticing his people out into the open country of the desert in order to kill them, or worse than that, another Pharaoh of the oppression on a truly divine scale. They will think God is a thug.

We see a similar concern for God's name and for God's reputation elsewhere in the Old Testament. It is a preoccupation of the prophet Ezekiel, for example. 'It is not for your sake, O house of Israel, that I am about to act,' says Ezekiel's God, 'but for the sake of my holy name, which you have profaned among the nations to which you came.' (Ezekiel 36.22)[5] As Nohrnberg remarks,[6] had he been able to, Moses could have usefully quoted Isaiah 48.9 and 11, where God is heard to say: 'For the sake of my name I will defer my anger, for the sake of my praise I will hold it in, so that I may not cut you off. . . . For my own sake, for my own sake will I act, for how can my name be profaned? My glory I will give to no other.' Ancient Israelite society, like all the others of the ancient Near East, and many in our contemporary world, placed huge and far-reaching emphasis on the importance of honour, dignity and shame, at least for men. That is very plain in the book of Job, where its hero seems less concerned about the loss of his children than about the disappearance of the honour he was once accorded by his local community. Now Israelite theology drew most of its imagery and its imagination from the world of men of power. It is hardly surprising, therefore, that its God should show such concern for his reputation, and for what people think or say about him. We may ourselves think his anxiety demeaning, but that may be partly because values in our society are somewhat different. Certainly, by the terms of the beliefs and attitudes of Israelite society, it is a very powerful argument that Moses uses when he invites God to imagine what the Egyptians will say. By itself it is not likely to fail.

Moses, however, leaves nothing to chance. He reminds God of his ancient obligations. We might have expected him to refer explicitly to his promise after the Flood. For there he vows never to destroy his creation again, never again, in effect, to seek absolute control of events, but to allow human beings their power and their freedom, however they choose to exercise them, and whatever the cost. Moses does, however, pick up the language of Genesis 6.7, where God declares his determination to bring the Flood. 'Why should the Egyptians say,' he asks, "It was for evil he brought them out, to . . . wipe them off the face of the earth"? . . . Change your mind!' Genesis 6.7 has, 'The Lord said, 'I will blot out humankind . . . from the face of the earth . . . for I regret that I made them.' The first similarity is obvious, but there is a second one, for the Hebrew verb I have translated 'regret' in Genesis 6 is the same as the one behind 'change your mind' in Exodus 32.

Yet it is of Abraham, Isaac and Jacob/Israel that Moses speaks openly. His choice is not surprising, indeed it is inevitable. For God is threatening to destroy his people, and begin again with

Moses. His talk of turning Moses into a great nation picks up the language of the promises to the patriarchs, and particularly the form in which they were first declared to Abraham: 'I will turn you into a great nation,' he says to Abraham in Genesis 12.2. Genesis 12.2, of course, takes us back to the very beginning of the people of God, when they are but a glint in God's eye, and Sarah and Abraham still have no children. Just as in the Flood God returns the world to the watery chaos from which it all began, so here at Sinai God threatens to go back to square one and start all over again with a new people. Noah came from the world before the Flood, and Moses likewise is a member of Abraham's people. But just as Noah was an unusually righteous man, and so held out promise of a new humanity, so Moses' un-flinching loyalty to God might provide the starting-point for a newly faithful people. Such seems to be God's thinking here.

Yet such notions are absurdly romantic. Noah did not usher in a new world, and Moses' people are unlikely to prove any better than Abraham's, for all that Moses can knock spots off the Abraham of Genesis most of the time. Moses, however, perhaps wisely, does not accuse God of being romantic. That might have been an argument God could not have heard through the din of his rage. Instead he reminds him that a promise is a promise, and that the particular promises to Abraham were repeated to his son and his grandson. Furthermore, they were made unconditionally and cannot be revoked, unless, of course, God is one whose word means nothing. That last part of the argument is not actually stated. Moses leaves it to God to work it out for himself. It means that this part of Moses' argument is also, by implication, an appeal to God's honour and dignity. It is, if you like, an appeal to his *divinity*, to his very identity as the Creator God, the Saving God of Israel.

The closest we have come hitherto to such an exchange as this is Genesis 18, when Abraham pleads with God not to destroy Sodom and sweep away the good with the bad. The two passages have, indeed, much in common, but here, on the summit of Sinai, there is a lot more at stake. We are not talking just about the fate of a town and its neighbours, as we were in Genesis 18 (serious though such a matter is, of course). We are not even dealing simply with the survival of a people. God is threatening to rewrite history, to untangle the threads of the story of Abraham and Sarah and their longings for a child, so late fulfilled; of Isaac and his coming so near to sacrifice; of Jacob and his encounter at Beth-El, or his wrestling with him through the dark hours at the Jabbok; of Joseph and his extraordinary rise to power; of those titanic struggles with Pharaoh, and the crossing of the sea. All that God is threatening to unravel, to let the threads blow away in the desert wind. It is a remarkable moment. God is speaking of holocaust, and it is his own people that he is planning to destroy! Moses reminds him of that, too, reminds him whose people they are. ' "Go, go down!" God began, "For *your* people, whom *you* brought up out of the land of Egypt . . ." ' (32.7) ' "Why, YHWH, should your anger flare up against *your* people," Moses replies, "when *you* have led them out of the land of Egypt . . . ?" ' (32.11) Cleverly he both quotes him and corrects him at the same time.

His arguments work. 'The Lord changed his mind about the disaster he had said he would bring upon his people.' (32.14)

*   *   *

That is not the end of the story, not even of this particular episode of the Golden Calf. To the rest we will return in a moment, but in the meantime we must turn to Numbers 14. We might think it remarkable enough that God should once threaten to destroy his own people. In fact, he does it four times! Numbers 14 provides the second occasion.

The people are now close to the Promised Land, and the previous chapter tells of them sending spies across its borders, to report back on what they find. They bring both good news and bad. The good news is in the form of a huge bunch of grapes, and descriptions of a land flowing with milk and honey, just as God promised. The bad news concerns the 'giants' who already inhabit it. Typically the people are more affected by the bad news than by the good, and plan to choose another leader and head back to Egypt.

Another momentous decision has to be made. Ever since God first promised Abraham back in Genesis 12 that he would give his descendants a land of their own, and identified that land as Canaan, the story has been moving towards the land's invasion.

True, there have been many twists and turns on the way, many moments when it seemed it might never happen. But the purposes of God have not been defeated. Now the people are on the land's very borders. All they need do is walk into it, and God will do the rest. And at this point, at *this* point, they speak of going back to Egypt! This is much more serious than their complaints about lack of food and water, or about the monotony of their diet of manna. This new plan of theirs strikes at the heart of God's purposes, of his design not only for them, but for the whole of creation. For the promises to Abraham in Genesis are presented as God's reaction to the events of the first eleven chapters of that book, and so as his response to the failings of his world. It might not seem that talk of going back to Egypt is as significant as the making of an alternative god, and indeed it is not. Yet here also a very great deal is at stake. And we have to bear in mind the cumulative effect, both for God and for Moses, of such persistent recalcitrance.

For a second time God has had enough! Again he speaks of destroying his people, and creating a new and even more numerous or powerful nation from Moses and his descendants.

Moses rehearses his earlier argument about what the Egyptians might say. Only now he suggests it will not be just a question of the Egyptians. They will tell their neighbours in the Promised Land, and they will all say that God was unable to bring about the invasion. This time they will question directly the extent of God's power. They will laugh at him as a third-division god, incapable of seeing anything through to a proper conclusion. Moses' appeal to God's honour and dignity is more direct here, for the stories of the plagues in Egypt, the escape through the Red Sea, the provision of food and water in the desert, and the great theophany at Sinai, have all been concerned with demonstrations of power. If people were to say, if whole peoples were to say that those acts amounted to nothing, and that God's power simply drained away into the sands of the desert, that would be even more terrible for God than continuing to put up with the people he has chosen. That, at least, is what Moses hopes God will think.

Again, however, he leaves nothing to chance. Again he

reminds God of his identity. Above the plains of Sodom and Gomorrah Abraham attempted to shift God's focus, teach him new lessons in the conduct of justice and the maintaining of holiness. Moses is not quite so ambitious. He does not try to change God, just remind him of who he already is.

> 'So now, I pray, my lord, find the strength to act in the way of which you spoke, when you said,
> "YHWH, slow to anger,
> Full of steadfast love,
> Bearing iniquity and transgression,
> Not forgiving, indeed not forgiving the guilty,
> But calling the children to account
> For the iniquity of the fathers,
> To the third and fourth generation."
> Pardon, I pray, the iniquity of this people, as your steadfast love is great, just as you have borne the guilt of this people from Egypt till now.' (Numbers 14.17–19)

The poetic 'description' of God Moses uses here is a near quotation of words first heard soon after the incident of the Calf in Exodus 34.6–7. They recur in varying forms in many places in the Old Testament. This is the second occasion. They have a clear formulaic quality, which explains why their last four lines do not fit Moses' argument. If he uses the formula at all, he must use it, so it seems, or at least summarize it, in its entirety. So he must speak of calling children to account, and of not forgiving the guilty, although forgiving the guilty is precisely what he is advocating. He means God to ignore the strict demands of justice. He has been ignoring them so far, so let him continue! Let him pardon his people. Let love and loyalty prevail! Mercy instead of justice. Or mercy before justice. We are very close here to Abraham's remarkable argument in Genesis 18.

The God of Genesis, when it came to the point in chapter 19, could not take it. With the stink of Sodom in his nostrils, he found the need to punish the guilty too compelling. So now. God's immediate response to Moses is to say, 'I grant pardon, as you have asked', and he concedes that he will not utterly destroy his people; he will not start all over again with Moses. That, of course, is a concession of vast significance. On the most important point, Moses has succeeded in persuading him to change tack, and has rescued the people from the flames. But he has not put out the fire. Having given ground, God immediately turns to talk of punishment. He declares that the whole generation that came out of Egypt, with the sole exceptions of Joshua and Caleb, will die in the desert, and only their children will enter the Promised Land. For forty years the people will bear their own iniquity – God will no longer bear it for them – and will know God's hostility (14.20–35).

Perhaps Moses *did* want to change God. If so he has failed.

Nor will he succeed in the rest of Numbers. In chapter 16 rebel leaders emerge who try to establish a people of their own.[7] If God will not do it, then they will! They accuse Moses and Aaron of playing high and mighty (16.3). Their accusation reminds us of the charge of that quarrelsome Israelite in Egypt against Moses, 'Who set you up as a prince and judge over us?' (Exodus 2.14) They also take nostalgia to quite absurd lengths by referring to *Egypt* as a land flowing with milk and honey (16.13). Moses and Aaron are the first to confront the rebels this time, for they are the ones presented with the challenge. But when God comes on the scene, almost predictably by now he threatens to consume the entire people, except for Moses and Aaron. The two brothers fall prostrate before him and cry, 'O God, God of the spirits of all flesh, one man sins, and will you pour your fury on the whole people?' (16.22) This is almost precisely Abraham's question about Sodom, except there the balance between the bad and the good was quite different. Moses and Aaron have nothing more to say, yet they have more success than Abraham did. God punishes the rebel leaders and their associates, and no-one else.

Not, that is, till the next day and the rebellion among the people spreads. 'Move aside from this community,' God cries to Moses and Aaron, 'that I may consume them in a moment!' (16.45) They fall prostrate once again, but this time we hear no prayer. There seems no time for that any more. The wrath of God is already doing its ugly work. Instead, Moses tells Aaron to conduct an urgent ritual of atonement. The ritual is effective in the end, but not before fourteen thousand and seven hundred people are dead.

Where, we might ask, does all this talk of God's violence come from? Clearly from the world of men of power, the world of men of absolute and ruthless power, who demand unswerving loyalty, and are quick to punish most terribly those who dare disobey them. The ancient Israelites and the author or authors of these narratives knew such rulers well, or were familiar with the memories of them. We have already observed that these stories of the periods in Egypt and the desert are closely concerned with demonstrations of power. It was perhaps inevitable, given both their experience of the exercise of power, and their knowledge of the mythologies of the surrounding cultures, also, that the storytellers should portray their God in the way they do. To explain, however, is not to condone or support. In the light of the Cross and of our own encounters with God we have to say they made a fearful mistake.

*   *   *

We might conclude from all this that God in these narratives is always the destroyer, while Moses always strives to be the peacemaker. That is not entirely so. If we return to the incident of the Golden Calf, we discover that the portrayal of Moses could also draw upon the model of the ruthless dictator. For there we find Moses the slaughterer.

Having soothed God's face and snatched the people from the furnace of God's anger, Moses descends the mountain to examine for himself what God has already seen. He watches the people dancing round the Calf, and now it is time for his anger to boil over. He smashes the tablets bearing the words of God, destroys the image of the calf, angrily questions his brother, and then cries, 'Who is for YHWH? To me!' (Exodus 32.26) It is a most terrible rallying cry, for he commands the Levites who obey it to take drawn swords into the camp and kill 'each man his brother, each man his friend, each man his neighbour' (32.27). To us it smacks of the very worst kind of religious fanaticism.

With the hindsight afforded by this slaughter, it might seem that Moses only sought to rescue his people from their God before, because he did not realize the true nature of their rebellion. Yet we have already seen that this is not the last time that

he will intervene, and indeed the episode of the Calf is not itself
yet ended. Moses' wild anger runs its course and then he remembers himself. He turns back to God, to make atonement.

The next day Moses said to the people, 'You have sinned a
great sin! So now, I will go up to YHWH. Perhaps I can
cover over your sin.'
So Moses returned to YHWH and said, 'Ah, this people
have sinned a great sin. They have made themselves a god of
gold! Now if you can bear their sin ... if not, then pray blot
me out of the record that you have written.' (Exodus 32.30–2)

Moses puts himself on the line here. He does not just offer to die.
He offers to be as if he had never been. He offers not just to
meet with nothing the other side of death, but to consign all he
has been and all he has done to oblivion. He offers to be
entirely wiped out of the story. So much for God's invitation
to turn him into another Abraham!

This offer of himself cannot be compared to his exasperated
cry in Numbers 11.15: 'If that is the way you are going to treat
me, then pray kill me ... that I may not look upon my
disaster.' Admittedly, he appears to distance himself from his
people, as he does in Numbers 11, by referring to them as 'this
people'. But in truth he is only separating himself from their
sin of making and worshipping the Calf. In Numbers his aliena-
tion is real, and his plea is made on his own behalf. Here in
Exodus he is courageously taking up the people's cause. In
Numbers 11 he is trying to escape from his responsibilities.
Here he is doing his very best to exercise them. In Numbers he
is not concerned at all with atonement. Here it fills his hope.

To Christians the method he chooses, or the proposal he
makes, is at once familiar: he offers to die for the people. We
recall those famous words of the High Priest Caiaphas in John's
Gospel, addressed to some Jews who are concerned about
Jesus' influence: 'It suits you if one man dies for the people,
instead of the whole nation being destroyed.' (John 11.50)

Jesus will risk everything when he goes up to Jerusalem for
that final Passover, and will, according to all the evangelists,
know precisely what he is doing. Moses risks everything here,
also, but does he know what he is doing? Might he, in fact,

have reasons for offering his life which are very different from the ones that drive Jesus through Gethsemane to Golgotha? Might he hope, might he believe his offer is one that God cannot possibly accept? After all, his earlier attempts to divert God's anger demonstrated such astuteness, such ability to read God's mind. Is he just being clever here?

The narrator does not answer that question. We are left to decide for ourselves. Perhaps the clearest clue lies in the hesitancy of Moses' speech, its brevity and its simplicity: 'If you can bear their sin . . . if not, then pray blot me out . . .' The first clause runs out into silence. Perhaps its consequence is too obvious to need stating. Perhaps it is too excruciating. Perhaps Moses dare not imagine the price God will have to pay for continuing to carry his people. Perhaps he prefers to contemplate his own annihilation, than to think of the breaking of God's back. Looking again and again at Moses' speech, I myself find no scheming in it, no attempt to manipulate the mind of God, only a stunning generosity.

His offer is not accepted, however, not, at least, for the time being.

> YHWH said to Moses, 'Those who sin against me are the ones I will blot out of my record. But now go, lead the people to the place I spoke to you about. Look, my messenger will go before you. Yet on my day of reckoning, I will reckon their sin against them.' Then YHWH sent a plague upon the people, because they had made the calf . . .' (Exodus 32.33–35a)

God is willing to give no more ground. He does not match Moses' generosity with any of his own. If Moses was bent on atonement, God is still preoccupied with destruction, so much so that his 'day of reckoning' seems by the end of the passage to have arrived before its time. There is no room for Moses to reply, no opportunity for further negotiation. In the end there seems to be no deflecting this God from his violence. Moses in this passage is magnificent. God is not.

There is something wrong with that, of course, but sadly something familiar, also. For too often still the goodness and forgiveness of God are made out to be far less than what we poor human beings are capable of.

4

So Near! So Near! Yet so Far!

(Exodus 33.12–23; Deuteronomy 34.1–5)

Exodus 33.11, 'YHWH would speak to Moses face to face, as one speaks to a friend,' and that clause in Exodus 32.11, 'Moses soothed the face of YHWH his God,' manage to capture in a few words the remarkable intimacy between God and this man. There is another passage, however, which explores the character of that intimacy, and in some detail. Given that the quality of Moses' relationship is unique in the Old Testament,[1] it is hardly surprising that when we turn to this passage, we find it one of the most memorable and audacious in the Bible.

It occurs after the incident of the Golden Calf, or rather forms its conclusion. It is precipitated by a twice-repeated command from God for the people to leave Sinai and go up to the Promised Land. He promises Moses that he will 'send a messenger' ahead of them, and that he will clear the land of its current inhabitants, to make room for them (Exodus 32.34; 33.1–2). This talk of a 'messenger' of God is still a way of speaking of the presence of God himself. 'I will send a messenger before you,' says God, 'and I will drive out the Canaanites . . .' (33.2) There is no change of subject, no '*he* will drive out the Canaanites'. Plainly the 'messenger' is God himself. Yet the way of talking is significant. In this context it puts God at one remove from his people.[2] For he cannot remain in their midst, as they move on towards Canaan. He is holy; they are contaminated by their sin of the Calf. The holy cannot bear the presence of such sinfulness, but must destroy it, just as light coming into darkness must drive it away. If God comes too close to his people, he will consume them. Twice he tells Moses that (33.3, 5). So he must go ahead of them instead, and must disguise himself in talk of a 'messenger'. For the time being the Tent of Meeting, which was meant to stand in the middle of the camp,

45

as a sign of his intimacy with his people,[3] must be pitched outside it. The people must stand and watch as Moses goes out to the Tent and disappears inside it. If they have a case to sort out that needs access to the mind of God, then they can come out to the Tent themselves (33.7b), but they cannot go inside. Within its confines God will speak to Moses with an intimacy that is impossible for the rest of the people.

When they hear their God cannot bear to be too near them, the people go into mourning (33.4). When they see the column of cloud at the entrance to the Tent of Meeting, the cloud that both indicates the presence of God and hides him from their sight, they prostrate themselves in worship. They are repentant. They have recognized again who is their God, and turned back to him. The damage, however, has been done. God keeps his distance. The tragedy of the broken relationship still weighs heavy in the desert air.

There is need once more for Moses to intervene on their behalf.

> Moses said to YHWH, 'See, you, you are saying to me, "Bring this people up." But you, you have not let me know who you are sending with me, although you, you have said, "I know you by name, and you have found favour in my eyes." So now, I pray, if I really have found favour in your eyes, let me know your ways, I pray, that I may know you, so that I may find favour in your eyes. See, also, that this nation is your people.' (Exodus 33.12–13)

This might seem a strange speech to come straight after the reference to God and Moses talking face to face as it does. It is awkward, certainly, and nervous, and full of repetition. Not what we have been used to from Moses, not at least since his great embarrassment at the Burning Bush. But we must recall the context. Moses has just emerged from offering his life to God, to make atonement for the people. He has just seen that offer turned down, and his heroic generosity matched by divine violence and the sending of plague. He has heard God put himself at a distance from his people. He has heard the sound of the people's mourning. He knows better than anyone, better than God for the moment, how vulnerable they are without him among them. In a profound sense they will be on their own, as Moses will be himself. A 'messenger' ahead of them will not be enough, even if that is God himself. They need God *in their midst*. And Moses himself needs the assurance of the continuance of his intimacy. That is why he says, 'you have not let me know who you are sending with *me*'.

He is dealing here with matters of the utmost importance, with a God he can no longer be sure of. No wonder he is nervous. Before Sinai, when the people started being difficult, God responded not with anger, but by meeting their needs. He split the Red Sea in half for them, he made the bitter water of Marah sweet, he gave them manna, he brought water gushing out of solid rock, he gave them victory when they were attacked by the people of Amalek (Exodus 14—17). Now, for the first time he has turned against them. The Golden Calf makes his anger understandable, yet we might imagine his violence quickly brings back Moses' memories of the plagues in Egypt, and of his own angry prayer in Exodus 5.22–3, when he accused God of being no better than the brutal Pharaoh.

What sort of God *is* he dealing with? He must see, he must know. The word 'see' is twice repeated in his short speech, and 'know' three times. Three times in the Hebrew we also have an emphatic 'you', which I have indicated in my translation by re-peating it each time: 'you, *you*'. He *must* have an answer, and it must make God's identity and character clear. God speaks to him face to face, but what lies behind that divine countenance? God has said he knows him by name. He has told him he has found favour in his eyes. He has paid him huge compliments. As Walter Moberly points out, the Old Testament nowhere else describes God as 'knowing' someone 'by name', and, apart from Moses, only Noah, in Genesis 6.8, is said to find favour in God's eyes.[4] God has put Moses head and shoulders above anyone else. But can he be trusted? Are his compliments too ex-travagant? Does he mean what he has said?

Did he not promise at the most solemn moment of the en-counter at the Burning Bush that he would be there with his people? How then can he threaten to distance himself from them? Did he not introduce himself at the Bush as the God of Abraham, Isaac and Jacob? Did he not promise to fulfil the ancient promises, and establish them as a nation in their own land? And has he not in a fit of rage, incensed by the making of the Calf, threatened to undo all that and start again with Moses? Moses may have persuaded him out of that, yet the threat was made and still makes the air uneasy. What sort of God *is* he dealing with? Can he be relied upon? Does he really mean what he says? Is it true that Moses has found favour in his eyes, or was that mere flattery? Moses must see. He must know.

Yet he is not just concerned for himself. He closes his first speech by reminding God that the Israelites are his people, and they will be the major concern of his second. In between God responds:

> He said, 'My presence will go, and I will give you rest.' (Exodus 33.14)

This will not do. Most of our English translations have, 'My presence will go *with you*,' but there is no 'with you' in the Hebrew. The omission is significant, a case of silence speaking louder than words.[5] How will God's presence 'go', and where will it be? God does not settle the vital question of whether he is willing to resume his place among his people, or whether he means still to keep his distance and leave them open to attack. He leaves things vague. And he only makes things worse by his, 'and I will give you rest'. In Hebrew 'you' singular is distinct from 'you' plural, as in old-fashioned English 'thee' is distinct from the plural 'you'. When God tells Moses, 'I will give *you* rest', he uses the singular. No rest for the people, it seems. Does that mean no Promised Land after all, despite God's assurances? Can this God be trusted? Moses still does not know. He asks again:

> He said to him, 'If your presence does not go, do not bring us up from here. For how, after all, will it be known that I have found favour in your eyes, I and your people? Will it not be precisely in your going with us? We are distinct, I and your people, from every other people there is on the face of the earth.' (Exodus 33.15–16)

Moses speaks again of 'knowing' and of 'favour in God's eyes'.

He begins by mimicking the vagueness of God's language: 'If your presence does not go . . .' Yet he soon makes himself quite clear. Unless God goes *with* him and his people, then they might just as well stay where they are and die in the wilderness. God playing 'messenger' up ahead will not do. It is in the midst of his people, or nothing: no Promised Land, no great nation, no distinct people of his own, no-one to speak of his special favour any more, nothing to show for his years with Abraham, Isaac and Jacob, nothing to show for all the trouble he went to in Egypt and at the Red Sea; and no new start with Moses – Moses has already refused that – no new start, just an ending, an ignominious ending in the desert. Nothing. Either that, or being in the centre of his people once more. God must choose. The ball is in his court now.

'If your presence does not go, do not bring us up from here.' Twice God has ordered Moses to lead the people to the Promised Land. Moses reminds him it is *his* job.[6] He makes it quite plain that it will not be enough for him to enjoy God's favour by himself. That must be extended to the people: 'how . . . will it be known that I have found favour in your eyes, I *and your people*?' He is, in effect, trying to persuade God that holiness and sin can mix, that light can accompany darkness without destroying it, that mercy can work miracles, and forgiveness achieve the impossible. He is trying to change God's theology! He is trying to alter fundamentally his understanding of his own holiness, or else to remind him of the promise he made after the Flood to live with a sinful humanity and take the consequences. We have already had cause to compare Moses with Abraham in Genesis 18, in the course of a discussion of an earlier point in this very tale of the Golden Calf.[7] So now, we must make the comparison again. Moses, like Abraham before him, is trying to teach God how to be God.

God seems to learn the lesson.

> YHWH said to Moses, 'This speech, also, that you have spoken, I will put into effect, for you *have* found favour in my eyes, and I *do* know you by name.' (Exodus 33.17)

Once again, in a remarkable way, Moses has changed the mind of his God. The compliments God paid him that Moses quoted

49

earlier were sincere. The intimacy Moses enjoys with God is real, and is unique.

Moses, however, is still not satisfied. There is yet more he must know about this God of his. He has agreed to accompany his people, but will his presence destroy them, as he has twice said it will? Which will prevail, justice or mercy? Will there be a miracle? Will the impossible be achieved? Will the people be able to live with their God, or will they only be able to die with him? Moses must get to the very heart of the matter. He must try to get to the very heart of God.

There is another reason, also, why he persists. The relationship between the people and their God is in desperate need of repair. It has come within a whisker of being destroyed altogether. Moses himself has brought the people back from the brink, but they remain, despite their repentance, dangerously close to the precipice. The stone tablets that Moses brought down from Sinai lie broken in pieces. The writing of God is smashed to smithereens, and can no longer be deciphered. What the prophet Hosea spoke of as a marriage between God and Israel (see Hosea 1—3), has come close to annulment, and Israel has been punished like an adulteress.[8] If God is to accompany his people and not destroy them, there will have to be a new beginning, a new marriage contract drawn up, two more tablets of stone engraved, and, surrounding it all, a new theophany.[9] Moses asks to see God's glory.

He said, 'Let me see, I pray, your glory.'

He said, 'I myself will cause all my goodness to pass before your face, and I will call out the name YHWH before your face.

I will show favour to whom I will show favour;

I will have compassion on whom I will have compassion.'

He said, 'You will not be able to see my face, for no human being can see me and live.'

YHWH said, 'Look, a place beside me. Take your stand upon the rock. As my glory passes by, I will put you in the crevice of the rock, and I will cover you with my hand, until I have passed by. Then you will see my retreating, but my face you will not see.' (Exodus 33.18–23)

This new theophany is to be a private one. It is for Moses alone. The people this time are left entirely out of it. We might possibly be alarmed at this. Perhaps God *is* starting all over again with Moses, and intending after all to form a new people from his descendants. The very next chapter, however, reassures us. It describes the making of two new tablets of stone, the establishment of a new covenant between God and Israel, and the giving of more teaching. God will remain with his people. He will still be their God, and they will still be his people. Moses *has* changed the mind of God.

Meanwhile he is to be granted a vision, which, in the long story of his extraordinary life, marks perhaps its highest point. In the Gospels he will stand on the mountain of Jesus' transfiguration. This vision on Sinai will provide his rehearsal.

It is all about seeing: 'Let me *see* your glory'; 'You will not be able to *see* my face, for no human being can *see* me and live ... you will *see* my retreating, but my face you cannot *see.*' It is also about 'favour' still, and compassion, goodness and generosity. This is the reassurance Moses has been asking for. God will pass by him, and what he will see is not justice, nor anger bent on punishment, but goodness. That is no vague, abstract principle. The Old Testament does not go in much for abstract principles. Instead God's 'goodness' refers to things like grain, wine, olive oil, flourishing herds and flocks, dancing in the streets, 'life', as Jeremiah most beautifully puts it, 'like a watered garden' (Jeremiah 31.12–14). It is just such goodness that Moses longs to see again. This vision will amount to a promise of it for the future, not just Moses' future, but, more importantly, that of the people.

When God breaks into poetry, and speaks of showing favour and compassion, he preserves the freedom to withhold them. He will show favour and compassion *to whom he chooses*. We may ourselves believe that God does not have such freedom, that his nature means that he can never do anything but show favour and compassion. But such a belief is not found in the Old Testament, and certainly not in these stories of the desert. As we have already seen, there is still much divine mayhem to come. Nevertheless, it is significant that *only* favour and compassion are mentioned here, and straight after the giving of the sacred name, YHWH, too. At the Burning Bush that name was explained, in so far as it was explained at all, in terms of God's being with his people in Egypt to rescue them. Here at Sinai it is expounded in terms of favour and compassion. That is what the name means here. Again, it is exactly what Moses and the people need to know.

The compiler or author of these stories very quickly came to feel that this passage gave a too one-sided picture of God. When the theophany actually takes place in the next chapter, and God passes by and calls out, 'YHWH! YHWH!', then to 'favour' and 'compassion' are added 'slowness to anger', 'abundance of steadfast love', 'reliability', a 'steadfast love' that will last to the thousandth generation, a 'bearing of iniquity, rebellion and sin', a very catalogue of hope and joy! But the list does not stop there. It goes on to insist that God will not forgive the guilty, but will call the children to account for the iniquity of their fathers till the third and fourth generation (34.6–7).[10] An encouraging imbalance remains. The vast bulk of the talk is still about mercy above justice, and God's steadfast love will last for ever, while punishment will reach only the third or fourth generation. Nevertheless, the insistence that God cannot acquit the guilty is very strong. In the earlier announcement of the vision, that insistence is not present. There is no talk of punishment anywhere. Goodness, favour, compassion alone occupy the stage of God's speech.

The language may be about seeing, but what will Moses see, when God passes by? That question is not answered when the theophany arrives in chapter 34, for that is less audacious and colourful than the announcement of the vision here in 33. In some ways the anticipation in 33 does not hold out as much as we might have expected for one who has been speaking to God 'face to face'. Surely he has seen God's face already. Why then should he be denied it now? But 'face to face' is a somewhat indeterminate phrase, indicating great intimacy, certainly, but not necessarily describing an encounter with the complete fullness of the divine. That fullness is what Moses has dared to ask to see. Even to him such a request cannot be granted. For an encounter of that kind is outside human experience. The Bible, both its Old and New Testaments, is quite clear on that. So are we. For a moment we may touch God's coat tails, feel the breath of God upon our necks or our cheeks, catch the scent of God in the air, hear the echo of her voice, maybe even know the warmth of her embrace. But those very moments when we know most profoundly the presence of God are also the moments when we are most keenly aware of her elusiveness and her abiding mystery. Only after death, if Paul's magnificent words in 1 Corinthians 13.8–12 are to be believed, will that mystery be dissolved, and we will see God entirely as she is.

Meanwhile, what Moses is promised on the rock of Sinai is the best we can hope for. Moses is back in the Garden of Eden here, and we have returned to its language. The man and woman in the Garden were created from God's intimacy, they heard his footsteps, they saw him stitching clothes for them to wear in the cold of the world outside. Now Moses is to be placed by God in a crevice of the rock; he is to have God's 'hand' laid over him, to shield him from the full glare of his glory; he will see God's 'retreating'.[11] The language is that of the storyteller or poet at its most striking and its most beautiful. Whole volumes of abstract theological discourse cannot convey what these few lines do. In the end they reduce us to silence, and we need to close our eyes, and let the images fill our minds and sink down into our souls.

*　　*　　*

There is more silence at the very end of Moses' story. This time, however, the silence is burdened with sorrow.

> Moses went up from the Plains of Moab on to Mount Nebo, the highest point on the Pisgah range that faces Jericho. YHWH let him see the whole land, Gilead as far as Dan, all Naphtali and the land of Ephraim and Manasseh, all the land of Judah as far as the Hindmost Sea, the Negev, and the circle of the valley of Jericho, the city of date palms, as far as Zoar. YHWH said to him, 'This is the land that I swore to Abraham, to Isaac, and to Jacob, saying, "To your descendants I will give it." I have let you see it with your own eyes. But you shall not cross over there.'
>
> Moses, the servant of YHWH, died there, in the land of Moab, by the dictate of YHWH. (Deuteronomy 34.1–5)

Moses is finally left behind, just when the people at last are about to enter the land. Without him they would not have got anywhere near it, indeed they would not even have got out of Egypt.

How are we meant to regard his dying there? James Nohrnberg claims that Deuteronomy 'insists on the fullness of Moses' life'.[12] He dies having fulfilled the one hundred and twenty years of the human lifespan as declared by God in Genesis 6.3; he dies with his old energy still unimpaired, and with the eyesight of a young man (Deuteronomy 34.7). He has given the Torah to the new generation of Israelites born in the desert since Sinai, to equip them for life with their God in the Promised Land, and he has pronounced his 'deathbed' blessing upon all the tribes. His work is done. He has completed the task that was given him at the Burning Bush. As Nohrnberg puts it, he is, 'humility incarnate', 'the man for Israel, not for Moses',[13] and we should not expect him to be granted, or even to wish to be granted, a foothold in the Promised Land. He is indulged enough by being given a view of the Land from Mount Nebo, and by being furnished with sufficient supernatural eyesight to see it all, from north to south, and across to the Mediterranean.

All that may be true, but neither James Nohrnberg nor the writer of Deuteronomy can prevent us feeling regret, or even outrage at this passage. The fact remains, Moses dies the wrong side of the river. He dies in the wrong country. He dies in Moab, and not in the Canaan promised to his people ever since the days of Abraham. Might not God have allowed him just to step across the river? Might he not have found the generosity to allow him to be buried in the Land, beneath a small piece of promised turf?

The question is sharpened by the unease of the biblical text itself. When we first hear that Moses will not enter the Land, we are told it is not because his work by then will be done, but because God is angry with him for not trusting him (Numbers 20.9–12). Though we saw in Numbers 11 that the relationship between Moses and God was under some strain at times, this refusal of God's comes as a complete surprise, and by the terms of the passage makes no sense.[14] At one point, close to Moses' death, Deuteronomy refers to his 'breaking faith' with God, and his 'not treating him as holy' (32.51), but that only points us back to the mysterious Numbers 20 and gets us no further. More significant are the statements early in Deuteronomy that God was incensed with Moses *because of the people*, and refused him entry into the Land on their account (1.37; 3.26–7; 4.21–2). We cannot help feeling this is the truth of the matter. At least, nowhere else do we find another reason that we can believe.

It seems, therefore, that Moses dies in Moab as a scapegoat for the people. We remember that he offered to die for them at the time of the Golden Calf (Exodus 32.32). At last, just when he is in sight of the Promised Land, just when he is within stepping distance of it, when his energy is still strong despite his miraculously long life, just at *this* point, his offer is accepted. It seems now, not the culmination of a life of service to God, as Deuteronomy would have it, but an act of divine cruelty that demands the most vigorous protest.

But Moses himself, the Moses who has spoken so much with God, and so very plainly, too, has nothing more to say. In this final passage about his death, there is no dialogue. Moses hears God's last words to him, and before he has any chance to respond, he dies.

What might he have wanted to say? 'My God! My God! Why have you forsaken me?' perhaps?

5

Hello, Hello, Hello!
What's Going On Here, Then?

(Judges 13)

This book, and our previous one, *Looking God in the Eye*, have been concerned with passages about direct encounter with God. The man and woman in the Garden of Eden, Cain, Noah, Abraham, Hagar, Jacob, Joseph, Moses. Those are the figures our books have covered so far. Only two women in the list. That is not of our choosing. It is the choice of those who composed the biblical material, and those who compiled it to form our Scriptures. There are no other stories of direct encounter between God and women in the books of the Old Testament so far which we have left out. There have only been the two, the stories of the Garden and Hagar ... and the next is here in Judges 13.

It will be the last, in the Old Testament, at least. Hannah will pray for a child in 1 Samuel 1, and YHWH will 'remember' her, but her story will concentrate on her relationships with her husband, Elkanah, with the priest Eli, with Elkanah's other wife, Peninnah, and the son who is born to her, Samuel. God will stay in the wings of that story. He will not speak in answer to Hannah's prayer. He will not appear to her. Miriam, Moses' sister, is described as a prophetess in Exodus 15.20, and so is Deborah in Judges 4.4, 6–7. Huldah (2 Kings 22.14–20; 2 Chronicles 34.22–8), and Noadiah (Nehemiah 6.14) would seem to have been prophetesses of considerable importance in their day,[1] but God does not shake the temple for them, as he does for Isaiah, nor does he fill the sky with the sound and brilliance of his coming, as he does for the exiled Ezekiel. After this story of the wife of Manoah in Judges 13, we will have nothing more to report about the spiritual life of women. In our final chapter we will examine parts of the book of Job. Job's wife will be given only one speech to deliver, of just six words in the Hebrew, and those will not be addressed to God. Near the end of the book God will appear in what is one of the very brightest visions of the Bible. But he will appear only to Job. There will be no mention of his wife. We will have to wait till the New Testament and the annunciation to Mary of Nazareth in Luke, or the meeting of Mary of Magdala and the risen Christ, before we reach any further stories of the kind we have been looking at, where a woman is centre stage.

The dearth of stories about women's encounters with God tells a sorry tale about the kind of society from which the Bible emerged. It does not indicate, of course, the barrenness of women's spiritual life, nor God's indifference towards them. Far from it. It is just that the stories of women are left untold, or unremembered, as still too often they are in the Church even today, thousands of years later.

The matter, the matter with the Bible, could be even worse than I have represented it. For the identity of the stranger that Manoah's wife meets in Judges 13 is not entirely clear. One commentator, Karel van der Toorn, asks whether he is not simply a prophet, a human messenger of God.[2] In reading the story in those terms van der Toorn is in a minority, and seems to us to be deceived by the mischievous talk of Manoah's wife in 13.6 and 10 (we will come to that later), but almost all scholars speak of meetings with 'an angel', rather than with God himself. We shall have to see for ourselves. The uncertainty can only add piquancy to our exploration of the passage, though we will pick up some clues long before we reach the end.

There are other questions we will need to face. How is this story to be read? With what tone of voice, with what look in the eye? The passage is like a musical score, and we, the readers and interpreters of it, are its performers. Only the page has no marks upon it beyond the 'notes' of the words themselves. There is nothing about the scoring. Is it for chamber choir, or jazz group? There are no performance directions. Should we play it *delicatamente*, or *con brio*, delicately, or with vigour, *serioso*, or *scherzoso*, seriously, or playfully? There are not many 'singers', four including the narrator. Clearly a male voice for

Manoah, and a female one for his wife. The mysterious stranger presents problems, but *so does the narrator*. Is that part to be given to a male voice, or should it be a female one? Might this possibly be a women's story? Might we catch the strains of women's voices here? A good case can be made for The Song of Songs, the book of Ruth, Proverbs 1—9, parts of Lamentations, the song in Exodus 15, and the story of Shiphrah and Puah in Exodus 1 having originated in women's circles. Other passages, such as the chant of the women in 1 Samuel 18.7, or the oracle delivered by the prophetess, Huldah, in 2 Kings 22.15–20, the teaching of the unnamed mother of King Lemuel in Proverbs 31, or the Song of Deborah in Judges 5, are actually presented as having come from women.[3] As we shall see, it is by no means inconceivable that the story in Judges 13 was first told by a woman, even though it has become part of a larger narrative composed almost entirely by men, and itself will have been given its final shape by one of those male authors. Yet, in truth, however we answer the historical question about the story's origins, we can still, as contemporary readers, see what happens if we imagine a woman taking the narrator's part. We can see what happens to our understanding of the story, to the way we hear it, to what we find in it, and to how we are affected by it.

The story comes nearly two-thirds of the way through the book of Judges. According to the larger narrative the Israelite tribes have entered the Promised Land. By the end of the book of Joshua they seem to have conquered it. But Judges tells a different tale. The process of occupation is far from complete. The peoples already occupying the land, or surrounding it, are far from happy with the invasion of the newcomers from Egypt, and far from unsuccessful in resisting them. Again and again the Israelites are overcome, always, according to the text, because of their disloyalty towards YHWH and their worship of other rival gods. Again and again YHWH empowers one of their number, a 'judge', to rescue them, but the people repeatedly lapse back into their old ways, and another crisis overtakes them. Judges 13 is set against the background of a particularly critical point in the tribes' history, and tells the story of the conception and birth of the last of the judges, Samson.

The chapter begins by sketching the background with the minimum of strokes of the pen:

> The children of Israel once again did what was evil in the sight of YHWH, and YHWH gave them into the hand of the Philistines for forty years. (13.1)

This is the first time in the Bible that the extent of the danger from the Philistines has become apparent. Occupants of the southern coast of Palestine, and lenders of their name to the region from ancient times ('Palestine' comes from 'Philistine'), the Philistines will be presented in the narrative as the main threat to Israelite security till their conquest by David in 2 Samuel 5. The story of Manoah's wife and the birth of Samson occurs, therefore, at a crucial point not just in the tale of the tribes in the book of Judges, but in the great story of the people of Israel that stretches all the way from Genesis to the end of 2 Kings. It can thus be compared to the stories of Shiphrah and Puah and the other women of Exodus 1—2, which introduce the long period of terror in Egypt; to the story of Rahab in Joshua 2 that comes at the start of the conquest of the Promised Land; to the story of Hannah in 1 Samuel 1—2, which begins the tale of Samuel and the establishment of monarchy in Israel; to the one of Bathsheba in 2 Samuel 11, which marks the watershed in the career of David.

Back in Judges 6—8 the enemy of the moment is Midian. Then Gideon comes to the rescue, and his story begins with an appearance to him of 'a messenger of YHWH'. The identity of that 'messenger' is revealed almost at once. Just two verses after his arrival on the scene, it becomes clear he is again YHWH himself: 'YHWH turned towards [Gideon] and said...'. (6.14) YHWH has not arrived unannounced on stage in the previous verse. Clearly 'a messenger of YHWH' is just the roundabout way of speaking of God himself that we have got used to by now. Here in Judges 13 'a messenger of YHWH' appears once again, but this time, as with Hagar in the desert, or Jacob at the Jabbok, we will have to wait a while before we are sure who we are dealing with.

Now there was a certain man from Zorah, of the Danite clan, named Manoah. His wife was barren. She had no children. A messenger of YHWH appeared to the woman, and said to her, 'Excuse me. You are barren and have had no children. Yet you will be pregnant and will have a son. Now, you must take heed, please. Do not drink wine, or any alcohol. Do not eat any unclean food. For see, you are pregnant, and you shall have a son. No razor shall come upon his head, for the boy is to be a Nazirite to God from the womb. He is the one who will begin to save Israel from the hand of the Philistines.' (13.2–5)

The language at the very start of this passage is extremely sparse. We are told very little about Manoah, but enough to establish him as a person of no recognized consequence. The narrator's calling him 'a certain man' suggests that,[4] and the description of his tribe as just a 'clan', and the lack of any mention of his ancestors confirm it. Yet Gideon, the hero of chapters 6—8, also came from very lowly beginnings (see 6.15), and later, in 1 Samuel 16, David, from an obscure family in an obscure village, will seem at first such an unlikely choice for leadership, that he will be left minding the sheep as his elder brothers are paraded before Samuel, the king-maker. Will this humble Manoah turn out to be another Gideon, or a forerunner of the great David, even? No. The 'messenger of YHWH' appears not to him, but to his wife!

The information about her is even more meagre: she is married to Manoah, she is sterile, she has no children. That is all. We are not even given her name. What are we to make of that?

Some argue she is diminished by the text, reduced to being a wife and mother and nothing else, turned from being a person in her own right into one who merely plays a role, and is 'a good little woman' in the process. So Cheryl Exum reads this story.[5] Others observe that her anonymity matches that of the 'messenger of YHWH', and point out that later in the story she comes to be called simply 'the woman', while the 'messenger' is referred to as 'the man'. Far from diminishing her, they argue, her namelessness and the lack of information about where she comes from exalt her, for they emphasize her closeness with the messenger and the knowledge and power she gains as a result. Thus Adele Reinhartz.[6]

I cannot help but find Adele Reinhartz's argument rather forced, but I am not sure I entirely agree with Cheryl Exum, either. Let us give the narrator's part to a female voice, as I suggested we might, and see what happens. What does the story become, and what tones do we hear? Does it not turn quickly into *parody*, with the sounds of playful but incisive mockery of the tales men tell about women? This story has already put Manoah in his place, before it has hardly begun. Stories told by women in cultures where they are treated as subservient to men often make fun of men and mock their ways. Storytelling becomes a means whereby they get their own back, have some mischief and find some laughter at men's expense, without suffering for it. Such properly subversive storytelling is still alive and well in Britain, and will remain until it is taken for granted that women possess the same dignity as men. Can Judges 13 be parodying those men's stories of women which do not even bother to give them names, or allow them any role beyond those of wife and mother? Far from supporting patriarchy and its diminishing of women, is it seeking to undermine it?

The story has only just started. We do not have enough to go on. As yet we can only ask the questions, and determine to keep them in our minds as we proceed.

Yet, however we are minded to answer them, we might well still find the namelessness of the woman disconcerting. We may still wish the storyteller had given her a name, to bring more colour to her cheeks, and make her easier to remember. Of the four women in Samson's story only one is named, and she is the only one everyone remembers, Delilah. There are several reasons for our remembering her, but surely one of them is that we know what to call her. We do not know what to call Samson's Philistine wife, nor the prostitute he patronizes in Gaza, and so we forget them. Here in Judges 13 we do not know what to call his mother, and thus we run the risk of forgetting her also, or of undervaluing her story, or of focusing undue attention on her named husband at her expense. The rabbis attempted to fill the gap. They called her Eluma, or Zlelponith, or Hazlelponi,[7] and since of those Eluma is by far the simplest and the easiest to pronounce and remember accurately, let us call her that. From now on this will be the story of Eluma and Manoah, and their meeting with the divine.

There is courtesy in the 'messenger's' words, more courtesy than Manoah will show Eluma later, a courtesy from which he could well learn, if he had a mind to it. The stranger begins by telling Eluma what she and we, the hearers of her story, know already. She has no children. She is barren, sterile, unable to conceive. He goes straight to the heart of her pain. The narrative does not speak of that pain. It leaves it entirely to our imagination. Yet that does not mean it is treated carelessly, as something of no significance. Old Testament narrative, including storytelling of the most poignant kind, is often extremely economical when dealing with serious or intimate matters. Think of the story of Abraham and Isaac in Genesis 22, and remember what that story does not say about the feelings of either father or son. There is nothing to stop us using our own imaginations in Genesis 22, and nothing to prevent us here either. In the kind of society in which Eluma lived, where women were married so young, where they played so little part in public life, where their bearing of children was thought so vital, where their rearing of sons in particular was deemed of such paramount importance, childlessness was invariably a catastrophe for them, and regarded as their fault, their failure, their disgrace. The 'messenger' states the obvious, yet in doing so goes straight to the heart of the matter.

His reminder of Eluma's childlessness could, for all his courtesy, be cruel, a rubbing of salt into her wound, if it were not for his next words. Those are so few in number, just *three* in the Hebrew, so unexpected, so startling, so gloriously nonsensical, so wonderful in their reassurance, words offering to Eluma new life and hope, and a prospect of a love, a dignity, a status beyond her wildest dreams! 'Yet you will be pregnant and will have a son.' The sterile woman will conceive! It is a nonsense, full of divine laughter. The childless woman will have a son! It is impossible, all topsy-turvy, too wonderful a gift for anyone to give her, except YHWH. Did not YHWH come in disguise to Abraham and Sarah, in their great age, to tell Sarah she would have a son, and did he not counter Sarah's cackling disbelief with an assurance that nothing was too marvellous for him to perform? History is repeating itself here. And what does that tell us about the identity of the 'messenger'? Is not *God* repeating himself here?

The son promised to Sarah and Abraham was to be none other than the bearer of God's promises for his future people. So here the son promised to Eluma is not going to be a nonentity like her husband, but will be the people's longed-for saviour, the one to release them from the crushing grip of the Philistines. For that momentous task he will need to be consecrated to God in a special way, not from birth, but from the womb, from conception.

There is surprise enough here, yet it is soon strangely increased, both for Eluma and for us. She has already conceived! Does not the 'messenger' go on to say that? It seems life is at that very moment stirring in her womb! 'For see, you *are* pregnant, and you shall have a son.' That seems clear enough, though, in fact, the tense of the Hebrew verb may not be quite as unambiguous as it seems.[8] What is certainly unclear is who the father is! Can he be this 'messenger'? Adele Reinhartz poses the question and has her suspicions.[9] Lillian Klein[10] argues at some length that he is, while David Bynum, bringing to the story a wide knowledge of folklore from all over the world, and of ancient tales of gods having sexual intercourse with human women, assumes he is. He writes as follows:

> Samson's mother, wife of the obscure man Manoah, poor woman, is not able to conceive a child in the modestly discreet way women everywhere generally prefer to manage that particular business of life, namely by a secluded act of sex pudently concealed against observation (not to mention the actual intrusion) of any third parties within the private shelter of a husband's and wife's own dwelling. Instead this woman ... has to go outdoors and meet another man [*sic*] who is not her husband in an open field [Bynum is, in fact, referring here to the description of Eluma's second encounter with the messenger in 13.9] under the full, unobstructed gaze of heaven not once but repeatedly in order to achieve her desired pregnancy.[11]

Bynum's remarks are undoubtedly very interesting, but in his certainty he goes beyond the text, and misses its playfulness. It is more discreet, and more ambiguous, also, than he is. Bynum tells us who Samson's father is. The text does not. It leaves us wondering. Soon it will leave Manoah wondering as well! Do we have women's mischief here, and the sounds of their somewhat ribald laughter?

Surely we do in the next part of the story, at least if we stick with a female narrator and imagine a female audience.

> The woman went and said to her husband, 'A man of God came to me! His appearance was like the appearance of a messenger of God! Truly awesome! I didn't ask him where he came from. And he didn't tell me his name. But he said to me, "See, you are pregnant and you will have a son. Now, you must not drink wine or any alcohol, nor eat any unclean food, for the boy is to be a Nazirite to God from the womb till his dying day."' (13.6–7)

So the 'good little wife' does not talk back to strangers, unless, of course, she is simply not telling, but goes and reports as she should to her husband! Is there more parody here? And does she hurry? Next time she does, in verse 10. Then she 'hurries and runs' back to Manoah. Here she just 'goes'. What are we to make of that? That the storyteller is simply introducing some variety to avoid monotony? Or has Eluma lingered more than she is saying? Furthermore, despite doing the 'right' thing by going to Manoah and telling him about it, is she deliberately leading him on by the way she puts it? She describes the visitor not as a 'messenger of God', which would clearly signal the presence of the divine, but as a '*man* of God', a phrase used elsewhere in the Old Testament to mean a prophet. Furthermore, her words 'a man of God came to me' could possibly be translated 'a man of God came *in unto* me',[12] and so imply sexual intercourse.

One thing, at least, seems clear to us, even if it will not to the obtuse and suspicious Manoah: Eluma has encountered the divine, and is genuinely overwhelmed by a sense of awe. When she attempts to describe the strange visitor, she struggles to describe what clearly defies description. Her halting language, her circumlocutions, remind us of Ezekiel's in his great vision (see particularly Ezekiel 1.26–8). She is surely struggling to describe *God* here. Talk of her encountering 'an angel' does not do justice to the brightness of her experience. In the end she will leave us in no doubt. Her final speech, and Manoah's, too, will confirm our strong suspicions: her 'man of God', and the narrator's 'messenger of God', are again but ways of speaking of YHWH himself, attempts to bring the mystery of God down to earth and within human imagining.

Yet see how convention has prevented Eluma from entering into dialogue with this God of hers! Whether her story is parody, or not, whether it means to support, or to mock, the constraints of patriarchy, it must have her speaking only to her husband. At no point in the story will she address God. Gideon, in Judges 6, did not have to go running off to his wife. He was able to detain God, question him, press him hard. In their dialogue (see 6.12–23) Gideon has more to say to God than God says to him. Nor did Moses leave the Burning Bush after God's opening speech to consult with Zipporah. Yet here in Judges 13 the only one to enter into dialogue with God will be Manoah, and he will not know what he is doing! He may be stupid, but he is a man, and that will be enough. There may be mischief and laughter in this story, but some of the laughter has a distinctly hollow ring about it. The gender issues are very clear.

Nevertheless, Eluma undoubtedly enjoys great intimacy with her God. He shows her great courtesy, goes to the very heart of her 'disgrace' and turns it all to grace. Just how close the intimacy is remains for us to speculate upon, as we have seen. If, remembering that this is the bright, audacious talk of imaginative storytelling, we do think of her and YHWH as lovers, then we are not going far beyond the poetry of Hosea or Isaiah when they portray God as Israel's 'husband' (see Hosea 1—3 and God's 'love song' in 14.4–8, or the exquisite poem in Isaiah 54.1–10). Yet Eluma is not allowed to be another Hagar, a woman who can talk with God and give him a name. We can see that Hagar was only allowed that privilege, and we the honour of overhearing, because she was far out in the desert and there was no-one else around. There was no man on the scene. Abraham was too far away.

Eluma does not tell Manoah everything. Whatever our speculations about her meeting with God, we notice a number of discrepancies between God's speech to her and her report of it to her husband. She has four pieces of news to impart: that she is pregnant; that she will have a son; that the child in her womb is already under a Nazirite vow, so she must observe its terms while she is carrying him; and that he will grow up to be the saviour of his people. She passes on the first two items, but she alters the third, declaring the vow life-long, yet missing out the prohibition about the cutting of the hair, while the fourth one she omits altogether, despite its momentous significance. Instead of reporting the prediction of her son's military exploits, she speaks only of his death: 'for the boy is to be a Nazirite to God from the womb till his dying day'. Is she so overcome that she is making mistakes? Is she indulging in some deliberate and mischievous misreporting at her husband's expense? Or has God's wisdom rubbed off on her? Does she foresee that another woman, over whom they will have no control, will cut her son's hair, and that will mean the effective breaking of his Nazirite vow and will bring about his death? And is she prophesying darkly that his death will mark the beginning of his people's deliverance from the Philistines? We do not know, but if she is, then she is truly showing divine insight. For though Samson will scoop out honey from the carcass of a lion and will eat food made unclean by death (14.5–9), and though he will indulge in a drinking bout with his friends to celebrate his marriage to the Philistine woman from Timnah (see 14.10[13]), nevertheless his vow will appear to remain intact until he allows his hair to be cut by Delilah (see 16.17–20). And soon after that he will die, and in his dying he will bring the Philistines crashing down about him in such a catastrophe that they will not be heard of again till 1 Samuel 4.

Yet if Eluma does exhibit a divine wisdom here, she is not sharing much of it with her husband! Without notice of the requirement about the cutting of the hair, Manoah cannot reckon with its significance. Without the information that the boy will grow up to rescue his people from their enemies, he cannot begin to make any connection between his death and the Philistines' downfall. Eluma leaves him somewhat in the dark. His ignorance, however, does not explain his reaction to the news she has just brought him.

> Manoah prayed to YHWH, 'Excuse me, my lord, that man of God you sent, please let him come to us again, and instruct us what we must do for the boy, the one who is to be born.' (13.8)

In the Old Testament we only hear the prayers of men, with the single exception of Hannah in 1 Samuel 1.11. So it is Manoah who prays and whose words are told to us. They amount to a simple, but important, question: *'What's been going on?'* His wife has been unable to have any children, and here she is telling him about a 'man of God' coming (in un)to her in the women's quarters,[14] and she does not know who he is or where he came from, and suddenly she is pregnant and talking of abstaining from alcohol and avoiding unclean food! What has been going on? He wants to see this 'man of God' for himself! He acknowledges that God is somehow involved in the business – 'that man of God you sent' – but he does not seem to have taken in Eluma's description of him, nor noticed her sense of awe. To him 'man of God' appears to signify an all-too-human prophet. He gives God no praise for the promise of the child, nor does he express any joy. He says he wants to hear what they must do for the boy, but Eluma has already told him. In point of fact, she has only told him part of it, but *he* does not know that. His request is clearly a pretext. He wants to meet and challenge this mysterious stranger who ignored all courtesy and convention by barging into the women's quarters without so much as a by-your-leave, and find out what really has been going on. We suspect he suspects he has been cuckolded. He might be right! The story is laughing at him, and in the laughter we may again hear women's voices. This is a delicious tale, and not at all the kind of thing we might have been brought up to expect in our Bibles!

> God listened to Manoah's voice, and the messenger of God came again to the woman while she was sitting out in the field. Her husband was not with her. The woman hurried and ran and told her husband, and said to him, 'Look, the

67

man who came to me the other day, he's appeared to me!'
(13.9–10)

This makes things much worse for Manoah! It is 'the man' now,
not even 'man of God', and no description of an unearthly appearance, either! And he has not met with them both, as
Manoah prayed he should, but again just with Eluma! What is
more, she was out in the field at the time, all by herself!
Manoah had no chance of catching this 'man' sneaking into the
women's quarters. He arrived when Eluma was *on her own*! The
narrator rubs it in: 'her husband was not with her'! Did anyone
from the village see them together? Is the gossip already going
round the houses? And what did 'the man' come for, if not for
what Manoah suspects he came for in the first place? Eluma has
no news to give this time of any conversation, nor any new instructions for them to follow. Right! He is not going to sit and
wait for this mysterious stranger any longer, or waste any more
time on praying, if that is how his prayers are answered! He is
going to find him, and speak to him directly!

> Manoah got up, followed after his wife, came to the man, and
> said to him, 'Are you the man who spoke to the woman?' He
> said, 'I am.' Manoah said, 'Now, suppose it comes true, your
> words. What will be the guidelines for the boy and his
> work?' (13.11–12)

First we are treated here to the sight of Manoah trotting off
behind his wife, when the culture of his times demands that
she should follow *him*. Then he comes to the one who his
wife and we know is his God, calls him 'the man', and asks
him a blunt question without any common courtesy, let alone
any sense of awe. Manoah cannot see who is in front of his
eyes. He cannot bring himself to use any politeness when he
refers to his wife, either. She is simply, and rudely, 'the
woman'. But he cannot sustain his bluntness when it matters.
He cannot bring himself to ask what he really wants to ask.
He does not say, 'And what have you been doing with my
wife?' Weakly he returns to the insincere question of his
prayer, about instructions for the unborn child. Manoah is
fast becoming a buffoon.

The messenger of God said to Manoah, 'Of everything I said to the woman, she must take heed. Anything that comes from the grapevine she must not eat; wine or alcohol she must not drink; any unclean food she must not eat; everything I commanded her, she must heed.' (13.13–14)

The narrator and God both put Manoah firmly in his place! The narrator reminds us, if we need reminding, that this is no man Manoah is talking to, but 'the messenger of God', and we know what that signifies. And God makes quite clear that Manoah's question is unnecessary. He has already told Eluma what to do, and that is sufficient. The commands are for her, not for Manoah. They are no concern of his. God is not going to give them to him, just so he can pass them on to his wife and use them to assert his authority over her. Indeed, Manoah's authority over Eluma is simply not recognized by God. YHWH has appeared, not once, but twice, directly to her, and she is answerable directly to him. Manoah, it seems, does not come into the picture at all, which makes us again wonder whether he has had anything to do with the conception of the child. To its very end the story never does refer to Eluma and Manoah having sexual intercourse. We are further encouraged here to regard this as a subversive tale, one that undermines notions of the power of a husband over a wife, and seeks to do so with divine authority!

Manoah, however, is not finished yet.

Manoah said to the messenger of God, 'Let us detain you, please, and let us prepare a goat kid to put before you.'

The messenger of God said to Manoah, 'If you detain me, I will not eat of your food. But prepare a burnt offering, if you will, and offer it up to YHWH.' (Manoah, you see, did not know he was a messenger of YHWH.) (13.15–16)

The answer to his earlier blunt question has knocked some politeness into him, or perhaps persuaded him to try another tack. He still needs to know what has been going on. If he invites this stranger to a meal, then he might find out. For if there has been any hanky-panky, then surely 'the man' will not have the effrontery to sit down at his table with him – but if he does,

Manoah will have the chance to observe him closely and question him.[15]

If that is his ploy, it does not work. The stranger does refuse, but instead of running away with a red face, he stands his ground and suggests Manoah's invitation was inappropriate. A sacrifice, and a sacrifice to YHWH would be more fitting!

Manoah learns nothing, or, at least, very little, from this interchange. The question of the precise relations between the stranger and his wife remains unsolved. In fact, Manoah will never know, and nor will we. Still Manoah does not realize who he is talking to. He is in the presence of God, and speaking with him, and he does not realize! Abraham also, as we will recall from Genesis 18.1–15, once entertained God unawares. Yet Abraham did not have the advantage that Manoah has here. For beside Manoah stands a woman who has known all along, who was overcome with awe at the first moment of meeting, and who has tried to convey to him something of the mystery. But he has taken no notice of her, and has paid her religious sense no heed. Perhaps he has thought religious experience of any depth beyond her. Perhaps he has always mistrusted that famous feminine intuition. Perhaps he has thought of her at best as just a silly woman who gets carried away, while he remains the clear-eyed one, trying carefully to work out the truth. Or else, perhaps, he has simply been blinded by jealousy and suspicion. Whatever the case, the penny does not drop, even when YHWH suggests he might offer him a sacrifice.

And yet perhaps the penny begins to teeter on the edge of his mind.

> Manoah said to the messenger of YHWH, 'What is your name? For suppose it comes true, your words, then we can honour you.'
>
> The messenger of YHWH said to him, 'Why do you make this request for my name, when it is beyond telling?' (13.17–18)

'What is your name?' he asks. Jacob asked that question of the stranger wrestling with him in the darkness of the Jabbok. Moses asked it of the one who met with him in the fire of the Burning Bush. Is Manoah beginning to wonder? Is a glimmer of light beginning to dawn upon him?

If so, the glimmer does not become a flash when God gives him the answer! Admittedly, God refuses to give him his name, though that is itself a clue, as we know from the Jabbok and the Burning Bush. But he does say his name is 'beyond telling'. Surely that is answer enough. But no, not for Manoah! Manoah prepares the sacrifices, and offers them up, and still is none the wiser. Only when the stranger ascends to heaven, does he realize. Then, at long last, the truth hits him, and he falls with his face to the ground in worship and dread.

> So Manoah took the goat kid and the grain offering, and offered them up upon the rock to YHWH, and a thing beyond telling happened while Manoah and his wife were watching.[16] When the flame went up from the altar to heaven, the messenger of God also went up in the altar flame. Manoah and his wife were watching, and fell upon their faces to the ground. (The messenger of God did not appear any more to Manoah or to his wife.) *Then* Manoah knew that the figure was the messenger of YHWH. (19–21)

Even now, however, poor Manoah cannot quite get it right!

> Manoah said to his wife, 'We will die, oh die, for we have seen God!'
> His wife said to him, 'If YHWH had meant to put us to death, he would not have accepted a burnt offering or a grain offering from us, nor let us see all these things, nor let us hear the things we have.'
> And the woman had a son and called his name Samson. The boy grew up and YHWH blessed him. (22–4)

Many stories depend for much of their power and their delight upon a revelation and recognition of identity at the end. This is one of them. The character who comes eventually to see the truth is not always mocked by the storyteller. Think of Oedipus, or Lear. But Manoah is neither of those. He does not have their stature, nor does he have their power to command our sympathies and our grief. And, of course, Judges 13 is not high tragedy. It is not tragedy at all, but comedy, delightful, subversive, sometimes hilarious comedy, told at Manoah's expense from beginning to end.

His reaction to this particular revelation is not wholly appropriate. He is aware of the immensity of the encounter, and the rare privilege that has been accorded them. But he is needlessly terrified. He quotes his theological text books, 'You cannot see God and live', but he chooses the wrong passage. That one does not fit the occasion. He gets the wrong God, as well. For a god who would destroy the couple at that point would make a nonsense of all that has happened and all that has been promised. YHWH is not a God of nonsense, and keeps faithfully to what he promises, as all the old stories make plain. Eluma sees this clearly enough. After all, she has known from the start that they have been meeting God, and they are not dead yet! *She* is not the one who has got carried away. She has always had her eyes open, and in her final speech she takes the chance to demonstrate it to her husband.

And her child is born, and blessed. That he will run wild and cause general mayhem once he reaches adulthood is, for the moment, neither here nor there. For the moment this is the third story in Scripture and the last in the Old Testament that concerns encounter between God and a woman. Its rarity may disturb us, yet encourages us to value it all the more. And rare or not, this is a story to be treasured for its craft, its colour, its daring, its humour, its defiance, its profundity, its hopefulness, its grace.

6

Now my Eye has Seen You

(Job 38.1—42.6)

Our final chapter will be concerned with one of the most extraordinary encounters between God and a human being in all Scripture. It comes near the end of the book of Job, and does not begin till chapter 38. Yet we cannot go straight there. We must start at the beginning, linger there a while, and then tell of a few things along the way. Of necessity this chapter will be longer than the others, but we will divide it into manageable sections.

The Prologue – A Paraphrase

This is how the book of Job begins . . . roughly:

THE PROLOGUE OF THE PROLOGUE

Once upon a time, in the land of Uz, there was a man whose name was Job. He was very, Very, VERY, *VERY* GOOD. He was also VERY rich, the richest sheikh in all the East, with the perfect number of *everything*, sons, daughters (fewer daughters than sons, of course, since sons were regarded as much more valuable in those days), sheep, camels, oxen, donkeys, slaves. Oh, and he had a wife, as you can guess from all his children, but we won't mention her for the time being. He was *so* good, that when his sons and daughters had feasts together (each of the sons of this wealthy family had his own house, and they used to do the rounds), he would summon them afterwards to purify them, and offer sacrifices, just in case they had done something dreadful when they had had a bit too much to drink. 'Perhaps they have cursed God in their hearts,' he would say. Every time they had a feast he would do this.

73

Act I, Scene 1

Now, one day, up in heaven, YHWH was holding court, and the heavenly beings presented themselves before him. Among them was one called the Satan.

'And what have you been doing?' asked YHWH.

'Oh, just walking around on the earth, that sort of thing,' the Satan replied.

YHWH said, 'Have you seen my servant Job? He's very, Very, VERY, *VERY* GOOD! No-one like him on earth. I'm most awfully proud of him!'

'Of course he's good,' the Satan replied. 'Who wouldn't be, with all the things you've given him? You've spoiled him rotten. Take it all away, and I bet you he'll curse you to your face.'

'You're on,' said YHWH. 'Only don't touch *him*.'

So off the Satan went.

Scene 2

One day Job's sons and daughters were having one of their feasts together, in the eldest son's house. Then a messenger came running to Job. 'Disaster!' he cried. 'The Sabeans have made a raid! Gone off with all your oxen and donkeys, and put the slaves who were with them to the sword. I'm the only one who escaped!'

Before he had finished, another messenger came running. 'Disaster, disaster!' he cried. 'All your sheep and shepherds have been struck by lightning, and killed! I'm the only one who escaped.'

Before Job could say, 'What *all* of them?' *another* messenger came running. 'Disaster, disaster, disaster!' he cried. 'Three bands of Chaldeans have made a raid on the camels, and have taken the lot, and put the slaves who were with them to the sword! I'm the only one who escaped.'

And before he had finished, *another* one ran in. 'Disaster, disaster, disaster, disaster!' he cried. 'Your children were all eating and drinking together and a tornado came across the desert and the house collapsed on them and they're all dead and I'm the only one who escaped!'

So Job got up, tore his clothes, shaved his head, prostrated himself before God and said,

'Naked I came from my mother's womb.

Naked I will return there.

YHWH has given.

YHWH has taken away.

May the name of YHWH be blessed.'

So Job was still awfully good, and did not accuse God of anything at all.

Act II, Scene 1

One day, up in heaven, YHWH was holding court, and the heavenly beings presented themselves before him. Among them was one called the Satan. He was back to give his report.

'And what have you been doing?' asked YHWH.

'Oh, just walking around on the earth, that sort of thing,' the Satan replied.

YHWH said, 'Have you seen my servant Job? He's very, Very, VERY, *VERY* GOOD! No-one like him on earth. I'm even more proud of him now. Look what you made me do to the poor man! And for no good reason, too. But he's sticking to his guns. He's holding tight to his integrity. So I've won the bet!'

'Of course he's still good,' the Satan replied. 'People will put up with anything, so long as they have their health. Take *that* away from him, and I bet you he'll curse you to your face.'

'You're on,' said YHWH. 'Only don't kill him.'

So off the Satan went, and afflicted Job with loathsome, burning sores all over his body, that itched like hell, and kept him awake at night, and made him weep with the pain. He went outside the town and sat on the rubbish heap among the ashes and the dung and the rotting carcasses that people had thrown there, and sat scratching himself with a broken piece of pottery.

SCENE 2

His wife said to him (yes, he did have one, you see), 'Still holding tight to your integrity? Curse God and die!'

Job answered, 'You talk just like one of those foolish women! We indeed accept what is good from God. Shall we not accept what is bad?'

So Job was still *awfully* good.

Word got around that Job was in a bad way. He was so rich he did not have any friends in the village, but three other sheikhs came a long way (from three different foreign countries, indeed) to see him, to show how sorry they were and give him what comfort they could. At first, when they saw him, they did not recognize him, he was so changed. When they did, they howled their eyes out, tore their fine clothes, covered their heads with dust, and sat on the ground with him, round the rubbish dump, for seven days and seven nights, not saying a word. They could see what a state he was in.

The Prologue – The Playful and the Serious

Well, that, at least, is how I read the first two chapters of Job. Nearly all of it seems either too good or too bad to be true. The author, the poet who wrote the succeeding chapters, one of the great poets of the ancient world, as fine as you will find in the Bible, has taken here a folk tale that would have been familiar to his original audience, and has sent it up. That, at least, is how I interpret it. You might think that it is I who has sent up the story, and mocked Scripture in the process. Yet there are clear signs in the text, in the Hebrew text, that is, or even in the translations generally available, that we are not meant to take this Prologue to the work entirely seriously. After Judges 13 we should not be surprised to find humour in the Bible, though the humour here is much darker.

Martin Buber long ago recognized the unreality and irony of the Prologue,[1] and more recently Athalya Brenner has exposed its parody.[2] There is parody elsewhere in Job, of a dark, bitter kind.[3] In chapters 1—2 it is more playful and mischievous.

Ezekiel 14, at verses 14 and 20, is the only other place in the Old Testament where Job is mentioned, and there he is listed with Noah and Daniel as a model of piety and righteousness. But the Job of our Prologue is quite impossibly good! He is described, to translate, rather than paraphrase, as, 'blameless, upright, God-fearing, one who shuns evil'. Genesis 6.9 tells us that Noah, the only good person on a corrupt earth, was 'righteous' and 'blameless', and that he 'walked with God'. But Job is better than Noah! He has four stars, when Noah only has three, and he is awarded them three times, in 1.1, 1.8 and 2.3! Other exemplary characters in the Old Testament have only one or two. As Athalya Brenner says, 'Such a cluster of superlatives attributed to the moral and religious character of a single person is to be found nowhere else in the OT.'[4] So right at the start, in this land of Uz (which may possibly signify the country of Edom, to the south-east of Judah,[5] but which now cannot but remind us of Oz), we are presented with a person, not even a Jew, mind, who is too good to be true.

That impression is confirmed by the description of Job's household, and by his actions and especially by his words. Wealth was generally understood by the Jews to be a sign of God's favour, and a reward for righteousness. Here is Job with a 'perfect' number of everything, seven sons, three daughters, seven thousand sheep, three thousand camels, five hundred yoke of oxen, five hundred donkeys, and later three friends come who sit with him in silence for seven days and seven nights! When his children feast together he conducts purification rituals and offers up sacrifices, *just in case* they have sinned inadvertently or secretly. That by the terms of the Jewish cult and the Torah is decidedly over the top.[6] The original hearers or readers of this tale would never have heard of such a thing. This foreigner from Uz is more pious than the most devout Jew! His devotions are a parody of faith.

So are his responses in these chapters to the disasters that befall him. This may be more difficult for us to appreciate, because of what the Church and Judaism have done with them. In my retelling of the Prologue I offered an actual translation of Job's little speeches in 1.21 and 2.10:

'Naked I came from my mother's womb.
Naked I will return there.
YHWH has given.
YHWH has taken away.
May the name of YHWH be blessed.'

'We indeed accept what is good from God. Shall we not
accept what is bad?'

The first of those has found its way into the funeral services of
the Jewish synagogue and the Christian Church, and together
they are responsible for the 'patience of Job' becoming prover-
bial. The fact that these two verses are all the patience we see,
and are followed by what amounts to some *sixteen chapters* of
Job's often extreme *im*patience, seems to have been largely
ignored outside scholarship.[7]

Yet think for a moment what this man is supposed to have
suffered! The loss of his slaves, his wealth, his means of
support, his power, his influence and standing in the community, his dignity, his honour (and in a society that set such great
store by male honour and shame), his *children*, *all* of them, his
health. Only his wife is left to him, and he dismisses her in
summary and offensive fashion. The man has *nothing* left but his
tongue! How might we have expected him to use it? After
Cain's 'My ... punishment is too great to bear!' (Genesis 4.13),
after Moses' 'Why have you brought disaster to your servant?
... If that is the way you are going to treat me, then pray kill
me ...' (Numbers 11.11, 15), after all the Psalms of lament and
complaint, after Lamentations, after Jeremiah's 'You forced
me, YHWH, and I was forced! You have overpowered me and
prevailed! ... Everyone mocks me!' (Jeremiah 20.7), what
might we have thought he would say? What might we have anticipated from him simply as a human being of flesh, putrefying
flesh, and blood? Surely yells of pain. Then, though he does
not know what has been going on in heaven, the hurling of
burning accusations in God's face. Pain and accusation are certainly the substance of his many speeches in the poetic section
of the work that follows the Prologue. In those chapters we
hear an authentic human voice. In the Prologue we do not, not
from Job at least. We hear only a mockery of piety.

If the Job of the Prologue is impossibly 'good', the disasters that befall him are impossibly bad. Many of us are at times familiar with setbacks, even tragedies, that come one on top of another. Yet the events of Job 1.13–19 come too thick and fast to be credible. Four disasters is one too many for a start, for storytellers tend to work in threes. And when the messengers appear so very hard on the heels of one another, we cannot take them seriously either. Unlike the friends a little later, we are not reduced to silence, but to laughter.

And if the disasters are impossible, so is the 'God' of these two chapters. There were plenty of tales of the gods in the ancient world, including the ancient Near East, which presented them as amoral, or even immoral. They shocked the prophets of Israel and the philosophers of Greece. Admittedly, there was another story in the traditions of Israel about God putting someone through an appalling test, the story of his commanding Abraham to sacrifice his son in Genesis 22. But that story is altogether of a different kind. For all the difficulties of its theology, it will not let us go. We are compelled to take it seriously, to wrestle with it to gain the truth it must somehow contain. Not so with Job 1—2. A 'God', for all his being called YHWH, who causes such mayhem, who is responsible for the death of all Job's children and an unspecified number of slaves, who afflicts Job with a most terrible disease for which there seems no cure – and the text is quite clear, he *is* responsible for it all; the Satan could not have acted without his permission – a 'God' who does all that *to see what happens*, for a mere wager, knowing that Job deserves none of it, such a 'God' is not only repellent, but quite impossible to place seriously in the annals of Old Testament theology. We have in earlier chapters of this book, and in *Looking God in the Eye* also, in our consideration of other passages, occasionally found reason to argue with certain aspects of their portrayals of God. Yet never before have we found a 'God' beneath our contempt. Here we have.

These first two chapters of Job are written like a children's story. They belong to never-never land. They give themselves away through the amount of exact repetition they contain. In my own retelling I tried to indicate its extent. Job is described in exactly the same words three times; the two scenes in heaven begin with the same introduction and with precisely the same opening dialogue between 'God' and the Satan; the four messengers arrive to the same words and end their speeches with the same words; numbers are repeated in the list of Job's children and animals, and again when the friends arrive; 'God's' two closing speeches to the Satan are very similar to one another. Repetition on this scale is unknown in the rest of the Old Testament. Small children love it, of course. The 'perfect' Job comes from the stereotypes of their stories, the 'God' and the Satan from their childish nightmares. They are taught to be deferential towards their parents, most especially when those parents abuse them. Theirs not to question why, for fear of something even worse. Thus Job's two pious responses, so applauded by the Church and the synagogue, are essentially childish, the reactions of frightened children.

Yet we do meet a grown-up in these chapters. When Job's wife at last appears, and cries out her few words, we hear for the first time an authentic, human, adult voice.

'Still holding tight to your integrity? Curse God and die!' (2.9)

Now we hear some pain, some anguish we can recognize![8] This wise woman 'overhears' heaven, and quotes part of 'God's' second speech to the Satan in the scene immediately beforehand, as again I indicated in my own telling of it. And she tries to shake her husband out of his frightened, childish piety, and respond with some courage. She bids him grow up and look God in the eye. It seems at first, with Job's quick and misogynist rebuke,[9] that she fails entirely. In truth she meets with great success. For in the poetry soon to come Job will follow her advice, never quite cursing God (though he will certainly begin his poetic speeches with a curse), but coming so close to it, that when God finally appears, we wonder whether Job will indeed be destroyed. Those six words of Job's wife create a tension which will be sustained for nearly forty chapters, till at last it is released and all is well.

Yet there are other things about this Prologue we cannot dismiss. We are dealing with a highly sophisticated writer here, and a mischievous one, too. He seems to be playing with us, just giving us some rather shallow entertainment, and yet in truth he wishes to deal with the great mystery of suffering, and with the even greater mystery of God. There are certain things he wishes us to learn from his Prologue and remember, beyond that speech of Job's wife.

First, *Job's suffering is real.* Despite the messengers inviting our disbelief, the tragedy of it all is genuine enough. Job is much changed by it, made almost unrecognizable. We learn that at the end of the Prologue, when his friends come on the scene. Job's wife has already begun to take us back into the real world. The friends complete the process, so that by the time Job utters his first poetic speech in chapter 3, we already know where we are. Playful parody is behind us. We are looking human suffering square in the face, and it is truly appalling.

Second, *Job's suffering is not deserved.* For the moment Job may be too good to be true, and yet he is clearly not a bad man, and when later, in their own poetic speeches, the friends try to convince us he is, we do not believe them. He is an innocent sufferer. He is not to blame. Unless we acknowledge that, we cannot grasp the poems.

Third, *Job's suffering has no plausible reason behind it.* It is a mystery. Of course, the wager between 'God' and the Satan supplies a reason, only it is one we cannot accept. Job's calamities come out of the blue. That is how he perceives them. That is how *we* perceive them, for in the scenes in heaven the writer has deliberately undermined our trust in his credibility. In the poems Job will clamour for an explanation, beating his fists raw on God's door in the process. He will have to wait till God appears to see if he will make things plain, and so will we. We too will have to wait till chapter 38 to see if the writer can remove the veil from human suffering and help us understand. So far he has been no help at all.

Finally, *Job has not yet got near God, nor his truth.* Norman Habel points out how the writer takes us back to a patriarchal world, even a pre-patriarchal one.[10] Job the book is dated by most scholars to the period of the exile in Babylon, in the sixth century BCE, if not later still, yet Job the character lives in the world of Abraham, if not before him. We find in the poems of the book that God is given archaic names, El, Eloah, Shaddai. 'It is as though', Habel writes, 'we were taken back to the beginning, when mortals were first struggling to know God.'[11] In the Prologue Job may be particularly, even absurdly pious, but we sense he has not yet *met* God. His faith at this stage is cautious to the point of obsession (think of all those purification rituals and sacrifices for his children), and driven, we suspect, by fear. Certainly there is no direct encounter with God here, and indeed, in the world of the Prologue it seems impossible. Its 'God' is remote, cooped up in heaven. He does not walk about on the earth, as the Satan is able to do. He seems to have no immediate dealings with human beings, and does not engage Job in dialogue, only the Satan. Later Job will speak movingly of the friendship with God he once enjoyed (29.2–6), and yet we still sense that he has only heard of God by the hearing of the ear, and that is what he will tell us himself in his very last speech in the book (42.5). In the meantime, God's keeping his distance is one of the things he will find so intolerable.

Job and his Friends – Bids for Power

After this Job opened his mouth and cursed his day. Job responded and said,
> 'Perish the day when I was born!
> And the night that said, "A boy is conceived!"
> That day . . . Let there be darkness!' (3.1–4a)

That is how Job begins his poetry. We have a different character here. It is not simply that Job has emerged from shock. The frightened piety of the Prologue has gone altogether, and has been replaced by a vigorous defiance which will be maintained till God appears. The story-book character is now flesh and blood. This is someone we can believe in, and his words command our immediate respect. It is as if he has opened his mouth for the first time.

His first poetic speech is terrifying. He does not simply wish he had never been born, nor even conceived. He does not merely cry,

> 'Why did not I die new born,
> Perish as I left the womb?' (3.11)

Such words are fearful enough, but this human being uncurls himself from his pain and loss, and flings his 'Let there be darkness!' against the 'Let there be light!' of God's first act of creation in Genesis 1.3. He calls upon those particularly skilled in the art of the curse to rouse up the forces of Chaos to challenge the power of the Creator (3.8). Thus his first poetic speech marks the beginning of a Promethean struggle. It will involve more than a series of exchanges between God and a man trying to make sense of his plight. It will be a contest to see which of them is fit and able to rule the universe. It reminds us to some extent of Jacob's wrestling with God at the Jabbok. That meeting was significant enough. Here, however, much more is at stake.

Yet, of course, Job is not only bidding for power. He is also trying to understand his suffering. As Martin Buber points out, 'That everything comes from God is beyond doubt and question,' as far as Job is concerned.[12] For Job, then, the question becomes, 'Why has *this* come from God, this pain, this loss, this utter degradation?' His is no calm philosophical enquiry into the problem of suffering. He does not sit behind a desk in a book-lined study. He sits on a stinking ash heap, scratching his sores. And he wants to know why. Like Moses, like Jeremiah, like the psalmist in so many of the Psalms, he needs to know *why*. For his suffering makes no sense at all. He presumes it comes from God, for the theology of the Old Testament claims that things invariably do. He presumes also that suffering normally comes as a punishment for sin, and that good days and prosperity are a reward from God for righteousness. His friends all think the same. And yet he knows he has done nothing to deserve what has happened. He did not plummet into depravity just before everything was taken away from him. He was as pious, as careful, as 'good' as ever. We ourselves know he does not deserve it. What then is God up to?

Job's friends see the world through the filter of an equation: everything comes from God, and God is just; because he is just, God rewards the good, and punishes the bad; therefore those who prosper must be good, those who suffer must be bad. They cling to that equation like limpets. When Job starts calling up the forces of Chaos, they retreat at once behind their theology books. They open them at the page where this equation is set out, and they never turn over. Their books are large, folio size, if not elephant folios. They are so big they cannot see Job at all. They can only hear his voice. They are so threatened by what they hear, they quite forget what they saw those seven days when they sat with him in stunned silence. Maintaining their religious and doctrinal position becomes their only concern. They have no concern left over for Job. Eliphaz tells him he is only being disciplined by God and should rejoice at the privilege of it (5.17). It is a hideous thing to say, but its hideousness never occurs to Eliphaz. Bildad says his children must have sinned, and that is why God had them destroyed (8.4). That is worse. Zophar assures him that God is actually overlooking part of his sin, and he has only to renounce his wrongdoing to find a life brighter than the noonday sun (11.6, 13–19). At its best that is an expression of crashing insensitivity. Faced by Job's continuing refusal to bow to their arguments, all three of them become increasingly angry. Bildad and Zophar begin to sound like hell-fire preachers, positively relishing the punishment they believe is given to the wicked, almost gloating over Job's fate. Eliphaz preserves the equation with which he began by inventing a past for Job and turning him into a heartless tyrant of a man, who may not be beyond redemption, but who deserves every ounce of the pain that holds him.[13] These friends, too, are making a bid for power, not nearly as ambitious as Job's, yet real and disconcerting enough. They wish to imprison Job within the narrow confines of their theology, to force him to see things as they do, to think as they do, to *feel* as they do, even if that means reinventing his understanding of himself and his past. There are plenty of people around today who can testify to being hounded by religious 'friends' serving their own agendas.

To his great credit Job maintains his ground, and refuses to be manipulated by such rancid nonsense. At the very end God will tell Eliphaz that he is mighty angry with him and his two companions for not speaking the truth about him (42.7, 8). God will bid them take animals for sacrifice to Job, so that they can offer them up, have him pray for them, and avert the consequences of their folly (42.8). Thus the author of the book declares himself against them, and his long work becomes the most sustained protest in the Bible against those who would hold to their religious faith at the expense of others, against those who set such store by 'correct' belief that they are blind to the people around them, against those who go trampling all over the hurt and the vulnerable in order to 'protect God's honour'. Jesus will pick up the cudgels of this great writer in his confrontations with the scribes and Pharisees in the Gospels.

Job maintains his ground because his arguments with his friends take second place to the case he would bring against God. His is 'a religious concern with the acting of God'.[14] Testing his friends' equation against his own experience, he concludes God must be guilty, and grievously so. If everything comes from God, then he, God, must be responsible for the calamities that have overtaken him. If suffering is linked to sin, and he, Job, is innocent, as he knows he is, then God must be the sinner. When the suffering is as appalling as it is in his case, then God must be a merciless thug, with no justice to him at all. That is the only conclusion he can reach from the vantage point of the village rubbish heap. If he cannot be persuaded by the friends to believe in his own guilt, he must go mad, or else he must accuse God. Consistently, fiercely, he rejects the arguments of his friends. Remarkably, given the circumstances, he keeps his sanity. So he has only one option left. He turns on God.

Imagine Moses' prayers of Exodus 5.22–3 or Numbers 11.10–15 extended over some sixteen chapters and you have an idea of the character of his speeches. For the most part, however, those speeches are not addressed directly to God, and not one of them is in its entirety. Job spends more time speaking about God than to him. Several times in the middle of a speech he finds himself suddenly turning to him, meaning to look him in the eye and face him with his bewilderment and the truth of his pain (at 7.7; 9.25 or 28; 10.2; and 13.17). Yet still he cannot see God looking back at him, and so he gives up prayer, and after the end of his speech in chapters 13—14 returns just once to addressing God, very briefly, in the course of his final long speech (at 30.20–3).

Yet though he gives up prayer as a lost cause, he does not give up accusation. 'You come to heal me,' he tells his friends, 'but your medicines are useless!' (13.4) 'You come to comfort me, but you just add to my pain! Your words are so much wind!' (16.2b–3a) He saves the vast bulk of his accusations, however, and the fiercest of them, for God. His friends may be making things worse, but they are not responsible for the tragedies that have befallen. God is, or so Job believes.

He accuses God of hounding him, attacking him, mauling him. Against the sustained silence of heaven he shakes his fist. One moment he rebukes God for ignoring him, the next he berates him for not giving him any peace. In his most savage attack of all he compares him to a wild animal tearing him apart, and then hurling his carcass to the jackals; to a thug who smashes him to pieces; to an archer who sets him up as a target; to the commander of an army that rushes against him with battering rams as if he were the wall of a city under siege (16.9–14). God took such care over him, in forming him in the womb, bringing him to birth, in seeing that he grew to adulthood, healthy and strong! But all along he was rubbing his hands with glee, waiting for the time when he could play his terrible games with him (see 10.8ff.).

Yet he is not merely preoccupied with himself. Having drawn his conclusions about God from his own plight, he applies them to the world at large. His circumstances are not unique, he argues, not even unusual. God is a sadistic tyrant, a maniac of terrifying power who rampages round his creation, causing chaos and pain wherever he goes, and enjoying it. 'Blameless and wicked alike he brings to an end. If plague brings sudden death, he mocks the calamity of the innocent.' (9.22b–23) Far from being a God of justice, he actively promotes injustice by blindfolding the judges so that they cannot see the truth. 'If a country is handed over to a wicked man, he covers the faces of the judges! If it is not he, then who is it?' (9.24) Moving from the human sphere Job finds plenty of evidence in what we would call nature red in tooth and claw to support his case. 'Ask the animals,' he says (I turn to free paraphrase again), 'ask the birds, or the plants, or the fish. They will tell you! They will look at me and recognize at once who has done this! The evidence of God's cruelty lies in every field, in every wood, in every wave, in every inch of the tall air!' (see 12.7ff.) God overturns mountains, Job cries, and shakes the earth to pieces (9.5–6); he returns the world to its primeval darkness by causing the sun not to rise, and by shutting up the stars (9.7); he brings droughts and floods, tears down cities that none can rebuild, traps human beings in a prison of slavery and misery from which there is no escape (12.14–15). He is himself a veritable chaos monster!

Norman Habel makes clear the legal metaphor, the forensic language and motifs that are sustained through this material.[15] In his third poetic speech Job contemplates the prospect of his achieving justice. It is not exactly a happy one. God is his adversary, his torturer, and yet he must appeal to him for mercy! God actively promotes injustice, and yet he has to turn to him for a just ruling on his case! God does what he likes, and no-one can gainsay him. If Job were to issue a summons, he would probably ignore it, and if he did bother to turn up to the hearing, he would so twist the testimony that Job would find himself condemning himself out of his own mouth. His is truly a hopeless case (9.14–24).

And yet in that same speech he expresses his determination to undertake proceedings. His pain and his sense of outrage drive him on. He begins in God's absence to rehearse his case against him (10.1–22), and he continues with that task in his subsequent speeches. He might forfeit his life as a result. God might reward his audacity by killing him (13.15). But what matter? Life is already loathsome and death would come as sweet relief and put him beyond further torture (10.1; and see 3.13; 6.16–21). In 13.23 he calls formally upon God to explain to him the crimes for which he is being so cruelly punished. He challenges God to bring his case against him, and he is confident, for he understands his own innocence, that God will be convicted of gross injustice in the process. In defending himself, he will convict God. With a relish born out of his pain, he goes into the attack.

He casts around for support. His friends give him none; God is his enemy. His wife, who in William Blake's famous illustrations of the book is such a constant support to him, is nowhere to be seen, or is entirely ignored. So he can only hope that the earth that soon will receive his blood will cry out on his behalf, as it did with Abel, that some mysterious witness in heaven will appear to take up his case for him after his death, or else that his own testimony, kept on record in heaven, will one day be heeded and allow him to have the last word (16.18–22; 19.25–7).[16]

In the middle of his final speech he suddenly turns again to prayer.

'I cry to you for justice,
And you do not answer.
I take my stand before you,
And you pay me no heed.
You have turned into my torturer,
Assaulting me with a mighty hand.
You once put me on the back of the wind, and let me ride,
Only to make my success melt away.
I know you will return me to Death,
To the house of meeting for all those who live.' (30.20–3)

It sounds like a final cry of despair, but it is not. Still no answer comes from God, but Job turns away and continues till he is done. By the finish he has sworn a long oath of innocence, submitted a formal, written, signed testimony, and challenged God to put his own case against him in writing and come out into the open (chapter 31, especially verses 35–7). In effect, as Leo Perdue observes, he issues God with a subpoena.[17]

Yet there is more going on here than an anguished crying for justice. As we have already observed, Job is making a bid for power. We said in our comment on his very first poetic speech that it introduced a contest to see which of them, God, or Job, was fit and able to rule the universe. In Job's final speech in chapters 29—31 he puts in a formal claim to the office. All Job's poetic speeches hitherto have been designed to make plain that God is not fit to rule, that he is the worst of dictators, and must be overthrown if there is to be any justice, any good order in the world. In chapters 29 and 31, he submits the case for himself. He describes the part he used to play in his community, and the language he uses is of great significance, for it is borrowed from the world of kings, or even gods. He, Job, so he himself claims here, played the part of an ideal king, who delivered those in need, and was showered with their blessings.

'I was eyes to the blind,
And feet to the lame,
A father to those in need.
The case of the stranger I examined.
I broke the fangs of the wicked,
And made them drop the prey from their teeth.' (29.15–17)

Justice and righteousness were part of his nature, his robe and his turban (29.14). Even if his own slaves had a case against him, he would uphold their complaints. By the standards of the Torah – and Job, remember, is not a Jew – he was blameless. By the standards of the teaching of Jesus – and Job is not a Christian either, of course – he was a saint. Apply to his conduct all the teaching of the Torah about giving heed to the needs of the poor and the vulnerable, and Job scores 10 out of 10. Test him by the teaching of the Parable of the Good Samaritan, or the teaching of Matthew 25.31–46 on the Last Judgement; by the sayings in the Sermon on the Mount on not looking on a woman with lust, or on going the second mile; even, perhaps, by the saying on loving one's enemies, and, if his testimony is to be believed, he cannot be faulted.

He speaks of having once walked by the light of God's lamp (29.3), then, not many verses later, talks of the 'light' of his own countenance (29.24). People waited on his words, he tells us, as for the spring rains (29.24), and when he was about to speak, everyone would fall into silence and be overcome with awe. Even the powerful would clap their hands over their mouths (29.7–10). He was the very model of a wise ruler, a paragon of virtue and justice. How utterly different he was from the thug of a God who now, he claims, rules the world! How much better the world would be, if he, Job, were in charge! He does not say that in so many words, but it is the conclusion he would have God and us reach. Leo Perdue sums it up with admirable succinctness. 'Job', he says, 'is the man who would be God.'[18]

There is a particular, and most terrible, pathos about Job's claim. Here he is, near to death, or so he believes, sitting among the refuse of the town, scratching his sores, the scorn of his friends and the butt of everyone's mockery, not just shaking his fist at God, but making a claim upon his throne! Whatever the justice of his case, his bid for power seems preposterous. Or are we to recall Genesis 1 and Psalm 8, and their solemn, joyful words about God's gift to humanity of sovereignty over the earth? Leo Perdue thinks we are.[19] If he is right, then Job is not just making the claim for himself. By telling his own story he is, in effect, saying to God, 'Look what we human beings can do! See how we can exercise the sovereignty you gave us! If you wish your universe to return to the good, the very good order and beauty of Genesis 1, then step down and hand over the reins of power to us!'

It is a challenge God cannot ignore.

Not God, but Elihu!

After the statement, 'The words of Job are ended' (31.40), we would expect to hear at last the voice of God. In fact, in the work as we have it,[20] we have to wait till after another six chapters! Those are devoted to the speeches of an angry young man called Elihu, of whom we have not heard before, but who seems to have been standing in the wings all along, waiting to get a word in, or rather, great piles of words. Someone, in Elihu's mind, must answer the charges Job has brought against God. Someone must defend God's honour and his fitness to rule. Elihu has been mightily unimpressed with Job's friends. Clearly they are not up to the task. So he, Elihu, will have to do it!

He claims God is unsearchable, but continues to say a great deal about him! He defends God's just rule and joins the friends in insisting that God punishes the guilty and rewards the innocent. To do that, of course, he too must demonize Job (see 34.7–9).

'Stop and consider the marvellous works of God,' he tells him (37.14). That is pretty rich coming from Elihu! (It may not be so rich coming from God, of course.) He tries through the force of his endless words to beat Job into submitting to God. He attempts to turn the defiant, human Job of the poems into the two-dimensional pious Job of the Prologue.

'Shaddai,[21] we cannot find him . . .
Therefore human beings go in fear of him,
Even the wise in heart cannot see him.' (37.23–4)

That is Elihu's parting shot. In the very next verse of the book
God appears, and Elihu will not be heard of again!

God's First Speech – A World Beyond our Controlling

YHWH answered Job from the whirlwind, and said,
'Who is this who wraps wise counsel in darkness,
With words lacking in knowledge?
Gird your loins, I pray!
Be a man!
I will question you.
You supply me with knowledge!' (38.1–3)

So the first speech of God begins. I call it the 'first' speech,
because we did not hear the voice of this God in the Prologue.
That 'God', despite his also bearing the name YHWH, was impossible. This one is not.[22]

Job's earlier speeches have included three long prayers,
passages addressed directly to God: 7.7–21; 9.25 or 28–31 and
10.2–22;[23] and 13.20—14.22, and, as we have seen, he turned
back to prayer for a moment in the middle of his final submis-
sion, at 30.20–3. Now, at last, the terrible silence is broken.
God speaks, and dialogue is established.

Job once rode the wind. Now it is God's turn. He rides the
whirlwind, like the storm gods of the ancient myths, like the
warrior God of Zechariah's vision (Zechariah 9.14), or the
awesome God who comes to Ezekiel in exile (Ezekiel 1.4).
Does he come to do battle with Job? Does he come, all
machismo, to batter Job to pieces? Will he fulfil Job's worst
nightmares, and reveal himself as the psychopathic tyrant Job
has pictured and addressed in his speeches? Will that challenge
of Job's wife, 'Curse God and die!' come back to haunt him,
after all he has been saying to and about God? Will he be destroyed by this encounter? God tells him at the start of his
speech to 'gird [his] loins' and 'be a man'. Are we to catch a

91

brutal sarcasm in those words, addressed as they are to a wreck of a man on an ash heap? Or is God calling upon Job to find again his humanity, his honour, his dignity? It remains to be seen. One thing is already clear. This struggle with God, like Jacob's at the Jabbok, is to be conducted through a series of questions and answers. Only this time there will be many more questions from God. God's two speeches here near the end of the book of Job are the longest put in the mouth of God anywhere in Scripture, beyond the declaration of the Torah on Sinai.

We need to follow the first speech to its end without a break, before we pass further comment. For it consists of a series of vignettes, and much of the power in the poetry is to be found in their cumulative effect. Nor can we make up our minds too soon what sort of God this is who has appeared to Job, or what the burden of his speech might be. We need the whole speech in front of us, before we can properly address those questions.[24]

> 'Where were you
> When I laid the foundations of the earth?
> Tell me, if you know,
> If you have the understanding!
> Who fixed its dimensions?
> Surely you know!
> Or who stretched a measuring line upon it?
> On what were its pillars sunk?
> Or who set in place its cornerstone,
> When the stars of the morning cried out their joy,
> And all the sons of God shouted in triumph? (38.4–7)

> 'Who shut behind doors the Sea,
> When he burst forth, issuing from the womb,
> When I put cloud around him for his clothing,
> Dark cloud for his swaddling bands;
> When I established my strict limit for him,
> Set up doors and bolted them,
> Said, "Thus far you may come, but no farther!
> Here will break the waves of your pride!"? (8–11)

'In all your days have you commanded Morning?
Have you told Dawn his place,
To grasp the corners of the earth
And shake the wicked out of it?
It turns like clay under the seal,
Like a garment that is dyed.
Their light is withdrawn from the wicked,
Their raised arm is broken. (12–15)

'Have you gone to the springs of the Sea?
Have you walked to and fro in the recesses of the Deep?
Have the gates of Death been revealed to you?
Can you see the gates of the shadow of Death?
Have you spread your understanding over the broad
    expanse of the universe?
Tell me, if you know all this! (16–18)

'Which is the way to the dwelling of Light?
Or Darkness, which is the way to its place,
That you may take it to its territory,
Or recognize the path to its house?
You know, for you were born then,
And the number of your days is so great! (19–21)

'Have you been to the storehouses of the snow?
The storehouses of the hail, can you see them?
I have kept them in reserve for the time of distress,
For the day of battle and war.
Which is the way to the release of lightning,
To the scattering of the east wind over the earth? (22–4)

'Who has cut a channel for the flood,
Or a path for the thunderstorm,
To rain on a land where no people dwell,
On a desert empty of human life,
To refresh the wasted wasteland,
And bring flowers to the dry ground? (25–7)

'Has the rain a father?
Who has fathered the drops of dew?
From whose womb has the ice emerged?
Who has given birth to the hoarfrost of heaven?

Water hardens like a stone,
The face of the Deep freezes. (28–30)

'Can you secure the fetters of the Pleiades,
Or untie the ropes of Orion?
Can you bring out Mazzaroth in its season,
Or lead the Great Bear with her cubs?
Do you know the laws of heaven?
Can you set up its order on earth? (31–3)

'Can you raise your voice to the storm clouds,
For a torrential downpour to cover you?
Can you send out the bolts of lightning so they go,
Or so they come and say to you, "Here we are!"? (34–5)

'Who put wisdom in the canopy of cloud,
Or gave understanding to my pavilion of storm?
Who has the wisdom to number the clouds,
Or who can tilt the waterskins of heaven,
When dust pours itself into a mould,
And clods of earth become a sticky mass? (36–8)

'Can you hunt prey for the lioness?
Can you fill the appetite of the cubs?
For they crouch in their dens,
Curled in the thicket, lying in wait. (39–40)

'Who finds meat for the raven,
When its young call to God
And wander about without food? (41)

'Do you know the time when the goats of the crags
    bring forth their young?
Do you keep watch over the wild deer
    when they are in labour?
Do you count the months they have to fill?
Do you know the moment of their giving birth?
They bend,
    they strive to give birth,
        they open their womb,
            they press,
                they drop their young.

94

Their offspring grow strong and healthy out in the open;
They leave and do not return to them. (39.1–4)

'Who has let the wild ass go free?
Who has untied the tethered onager,
For whom I have made the desert plain his home,
The salt wastes his dwelling place?
He laughs at the noise of the town.
He does not have to listen to the shouts of a driver.
He ranges the mountains as his pastures,
Searching after anything green. (5–8)

'Does the wild ox consent to be your servant,
Or spend the night beside your feeding trough?
Can you guide him with ropes along the furrow?
Will he walk behind you and harrow the valley fields?
Can you put your trust in his great strength,
Or leave your work for him to get on with?
Can you rely on him to return,
And bring in your grain to your threshing floor? (9–12)

'The wing of the ostrich rejoices:
She has such gracious pinions and plumage!
Yet she leaves her eggs on the ground,
And lets them get hot in the dust.
She forgets a foot might crush them,
That a wild animal might trample on them.
She treats her young with disdain,
As if they were not hers.
Her work in rearing them may come to nothing,
But she does not care.
For Eloah[25] has deprived her of wisdom,
And given her no share of understanding.
But when she picks up her feet and runs,
She laughs at horse and rider! (13–18)

'Do you give the horse his might?
Do you clothe his neck with thunder?
Do you make him jump like a locust?
Terrifying is the majesty of his snorting!
Vigorously he paws the ground,

95

And exults in his strength!
He rushes to meet the fray;
He laughs at fear;
He is not dismayed!
He does not turn back from the face of the sword!
Upon his side the quiver rattles,
The flashing spear and the lance.
Trembling with excitement,
   he eats up the ground.
He can hardly believe the trumpet has sounded.
As the trumpet calls, he cries, "Hurrah!"
From afar he catches the smell of battle,
The bellowing of the captains,
And the war cries. (19–25)

'Is it with your guidance
   that the eagle flies
And spreads his wings to the south? (26)

'When you open your mouth,
Does the vulture soar
To build his nest on the high ledge?
The crag it makes its home;
Its stronghold is a sharp crag.
From there he scans for food,
From afar his eyes see it.
His young gulp down blood,
And where the slain are,
There he is.' (27–30)

God's First Speech – Further Comment

If we look to this poem to provide an answer to the problem of suffering, as some have in the past, then we will be disappointed. If we expect God to appear as a Good Samaritan, and tend Job's sores and heal his grief, then we will feel angry and let down, for he seems to pay no heed to his plight at all. But we have come a long way since those catastrophes of the Prologue. While Job has reminded us of his misery all along, right up to his final speech (see chapter 30), we have also heard him deliver a fearful heap of accusations against God, and seen him make an astonishing bid for power. We have understood him to argue that human beings could make a darn sight better job of ruling the universe than God. God must answer the accusations. God must confront his rival, and put him in his place. That is precisely what he does in this speech.

In the book of Isaiah there are a number of poetic trial speeches, where YHWH is pictured as summoning the foreign nations and their gods 'into court', to challenge their claims (see Isaiah 41.1–5, 21–9; 43.8–15; 44.6–8; 45.20–5). He asks the gods,

> 'What were things in the beginning?
> Tell us what they were,
> so that we can put our mind to them!
> Or let us know what is to follow;
> Let us hear about what is to come!
> Tell us what is on its way,
> And let us know that *you* are gods!' (Isaiah 41.22b–23a)

We cannot help being reminded of God's speech to Job, and the questions he poses. If we read Isaiah before we come to Job, however, what strikes us about the poem in Job is not how very forceful its language is, but how restrained. Of course God does not mince matters. Of course he means to refute Job's accusations in no uncertain terms, and show up his claim to sovereignty as utterly absurd. Of course he does not arrive on the whirlwind still wearing his carpet slippers. The trial that Job has set up, and the case he has brought are of the utmost significance. We can hardly imagine questions more important than what sort of God we are dealing with, and whether he is fit to rule the world, and whether we human beings could not do a better job of it. They are central questions for our times, as well as Job's. So of course God does not pussyfoot his way round Job's rubbish heap. Yet he does not put him down in the way Isaiah's God disposes of the foreign gods:

> 'See, you are less than nothing,
> and your deeds are worse than useless!
> Whoever chooses you is an abomination!' (Isaiah 41.24)[26]

At no point in his speech to Job does God attack him in such a manner. Indeed, he does not attack him at all, only the content of his speeches. Instead of verbal abuse, there is delight and room for laughter; playful sarcasm in places, certainly (see 38.21), and questions that put Job and the rest of us in our place, but no humiliation.

The God who appears in Job 38—39 is not nearly as macho as the one who disputes with the gods and the nations in Isaiah. If we take the trouble to notice the range of metaphors and images the poet of Job uses, we will discover something quite remarkable. Most of the language used of God in the Old Testament (and the New), and applied to him so far in the book of Job itself, is borrowed from the world of men of power. In Job 38—39 it is taken instead from the domestic sphere.

The questions God poses are perfectly easy for Job to answer, but just in case he does not get the point, God explains the first one for him: not, 'Who laid the foundations of the earth?', but 'Where were you when *I* laid the foundations of the earth?' So it is quite plain who it is who also tucks up the Sea in bed and lays down the house rules; who takes Light and Darkness home; who inspects the storehouses of the snow and the hail; who digs irrigation channels in the desert; who fathers the rain and the dew, or gives birth to the ice and hoarfrost; who acts as herdsman or herdswoman to the constellations; who gives instructions to the storms and the lightning, as if to slaves; who empties the waterskins of heaven to make it rain; who hunts prey for the lions in the dry season, finds meat for the newly fledged ravens, plays midwife to the ibex and the wild deer, unties the wild ass, ploughs the wasteland with the wild ox, guides the migrating eagle, shows the vulture a suitable ledge for her eyrie. It is God. It is God. The world, indeed the universe, is portrayed in this poem as God's household, God's farm.

In the households and the farms of ancient Israel the duties were shared between husband and wife, as indeed they are in our society (though not, of course, always with equity). It is not surprising, therefore, that this poem should include feminine images of God, and portray her as the mother of the Sea and of the ice and hoarfrost, or midwife to the ibex and deer. Many of the other images are not gender specific, either. Indeed, perhaps the only ones that are to be seen as peculiarly masculine, apart from the fathering of the rain and dew, are the ones of God laying foundations, digging irrigation channels, ploughing, or hunting. Feminine images of God are a rarity in the Old Testament, as we have already seen.[27] Their appearance here is significant, and further distances this God from the macho 'God' of Job's fevered imaginings.

Near the end of his speech God seems to get carried away. The depictions of the war horse, and the ostrich (a bird which incidentally takes far more care of its eggs and its young than the poem suggests), become pure celebration. We can almost see God shouting with glee over the horse, or doubling up with laughter over the notion of an ostrich flapping its wings, then cheering to high heaven when she sees it run! And this is the God whom Job accused of overturning mountains, of filling the world with his cruelty!

But where do human beings feature in this poem? We see the wicked shaken out of the world's coverlet by the housewife of Dawn, we hear tell of battle and war, we catch the distant echoes of the town and the shouts of those driving along their pack animals, we find someone riding the horse that is outrun by the ostrich, but that is all. The series of vignettes either take us far beyond human knowledge and experience, to the building of the earth or the gates of Death, or else lead us out into the wild where no human beings live or can survive. Perhaps the most instructive of them is the picture of the war horse. Nowhere is there mention of its rider. This magnificent animal has a mind of its own, and enters the battle purely because it relishes its noise and smell. The lines devoted to it spill over with admiration and love of horses, but say nothing at all about the arts of riding or soldiering. Job 38—39 is the great 'green' text of the Bible. It is the purest, the most sustained celebration of what we call 'the natural world' in all Scripture, and precisely because it does not put human beings at the centre. In many wonderfully colourful ways it echoes the vision of Genesis 1, and that poem's celebration of the good order and the beauty of the world. Unlike Genesis 1, however, it refuses to present human beings as the crown of God's creation. It refuses to give them sovereignty over the earth. Rather, it goes out of its way to deny them that sovereignty, because, of course, one of its main purposes is to disappoint Job's or humanity's threatened *coup d'état*. God alone is sovereign, or rather, God alone is the householder with the wisdom wide enough to order and sustain the earth. The idea that human beings could do that for him is ridiculous.

Yet that speech, marvellous though it is, is not enough. It may establish God as more than fit to order the world, and as the only one who can. It may answer many of Job's accusations, as well as deny his claim to power. It does not, however, adequately deal with evil and suffering. It only tells part of the story. Admittedly, it is not so one-sided in its vision of creation as Genesis 1, where *everything* is in good order and very beautiful. It acknowledges the presence of human wickedness and war, and most especially of Chaos, for that is what the Sea represents. But the power of the wicked is soon curtailed by the dawn coming to throw light on their dark deeds and frighten them back home. The terrible suffering caused by war is not given mention, either, only the excitement of battle. And Chaos is safely tucked up in bed, or told where it can go out to play, and where it cannot. If this speech were God's only response, Job could rightly accuse him of being romantic, and, worse, of not taking the suffering of the world and his own terrible plight seriously. For all his magnificent words, God could end up seeming blind to the harsher realities of the world, and, like the friends, blind to Job.

But this is not God's last speech. He has one more, one more, that is, before the poetry comes to an end, and the writer reverts to prose and takes us back to never-never land.

Job's First Response – Questions Still Unanswered

Before we look at God's second speech, however, we must briefly record the challenge with which the first speech ends, and Job's immediate response.

> YHWH answered Job and said,
>> 'Will the one who brings a case against Shaddai
>> Correct him?

Will the one who prosecutes Eloah
Give the answers?' (40.1–2)
Job answered YHWH and said,
    'Ah, how small I am!
    How can I respond to you?
    I put my hand over my mouth.
    Once I have spoken,
    But now cannot answer;
    Twice, but have nothing to add.' (3–5)

The poetry may be wonderful, but it is hard to hear Job here, and not just because he has his hand over his mouth. What is his tone of voice? Does he feel humiliated? The Hebrew word for 'small' could suggest he does. Or does it simply mean he knows he has been put in his place, and that he is too 'small' to be ruler of the universe? And further, though he is not going to proceed further with his case, has he withdrawn it? That is not clear either. All we know is that he has given up any bid for power. That is not enough. We knew at the end of chapter 39 that God would have to give a second speech. Job's reaction underlines its necessity.

God's Second Speech – Chaos and Evil Displayed

YHWH answered Job from the whirlwind, and said,
    'Gird your loins, I pray!
    Be a man!
    I will question you.
    You supply me with knowledge!

    'Will you really overturn my justice?
    Will you pronounce me guilty,
    So that you can be innocent?
    But if you have an arm like El's[28]
    And can thunder with a voice like his . . .
    Deck yourself, I pray, with lofty majesty.
    Clothe yourself with grand splendour.
    Scatter the furies of your wrath,
    Look upon any that are proud
        and bring them low!

Look on any that are proud
  and subdue them!
Crush the wicked where they stand,
Hide them together in the dust,
Bind their faces in the place of hiding.
Then I myself will worship you,
You whose own right hand has brought deliverance!'
  (40.6–14)

The language here is much more what we might have expected. It is the language of kings, of warriors, of judges. And yet this time God is not describing what he does, so much as what he *cannot* do! He is not celebrating his victory over the forces of chaos and oppression, so much as challenging Job to win for him the battles he himself finds so very hard. 'I cannot destroy evil, Job, so you have a go!' is what he seems to be saying. 'If you succeed where I continually fail, then I will hand over my divinity to you and worship you!'

Thus in a few lines the poet pulls out the rug from underneath all romantic theologies that would seek only to praise God as if all were well with the world. Thus, also, this God reveals to Job how very seriously he takes the power of evil.

But he is not finished yet. His second speech has barely begun. Once again we will proceed through to the end of it, that we might more easily feel the power of its language and imagery. But first we must say something about the two 'creatures' it describes, Behemoth and Leviathan.

The animals of the first speech were beyond human taming, but were still benign, indeed grounds for much celebration. Behemoth and Leviathan are decidedly not benign, and are reason instead for much fear. The earlier animals were all recognizable. Though Behemoth and Leviathan may remind us of the hippopotamus and the crocodile, they are not ordinary animals at all. Leviathan breathes fire and smoke and in the end makes us think of dragons rather than crocodiles, and Behemoth, too, for all we are told about hippopotamuses biting people in half, seems to be a good deal larger and more terrifying than life. We cannot imagine coming across either of them in a zoo, or hearing David Attenborough commenting on them in a BBC television series, even in his most reverential tones. They belong more to the world of myth than natural history, and indeed the mythologies of the ancient Near East would identify them both as symbols of the forces of chaos and evil that threaten the sovereignty of the Creator and the good order of his creation.[29] So if we translate Behemoth (almost literally, as it happens) as 'The Beast', and Leviathan as 'The Dragon', we will come close to their meaning and capture something of their terror.

'Look, I pray,
The Beast, which I made along with you.
He eats grass like cattle,
But look, the strength in his loins,
The power in the muscles of his belly!
His penis stiffens like a pine,
The veins stand out on his testicles!
His limbs are tubes of bronze,
His bones bars of iron!
He lies at the head of the works of El.
His maker approaches him with the sword.
The mountains offer him their produce,
Where all the wild animals play.
Beneath the lotuses he makes his bed,
In the cover of the reeds and the swamp.
The lotuses hide him in shadow,
The trees of the river surround him.
If the stream rages, he is not alarmed;
He stays calm, though the Jordan become a torrent.
Try to take him by the mouth with rings,
Pierce his nose with hooks! (40.15–24)

'Can you catch the Dragon with a hook,
press down his tongue with a line?
Can you put a rope through his nose,
Or pierce his jaw with a barb?
Will he inundate you with supplications,
Or speak soft words with you?
Will he make a covenant with you,
That you might take him as your slave for ever?

Will you play with him as you might with a bird,
Or put him on a leash for your girls?
Will traders haggle over him,
Divide him up among the merchants?
Can you riddle his hide with spears,
Or his head with harpoons?
Lay a hand on him . . .
Think of the battle!
You would not do it twice!
See, any hope of beating him is false;
One is thrown to the ground by the mere sight of him.
There is no-one fierce enough to rouse him.
Who is there who would stand before him?
Whoever confronts him I will reward!
But who is there beneath the whole heaven who could?
   (41.1–11)

'I cannot keep silent about his limbs,
Nor about his might, or the grace of his form.
Who can remove his outer clothing,
Or get through his double coat of mail?
Who can open the doors of his face,
When his teeth surround it with terror?
His back is a row of shields,
Shut, and sealed tight.
One is so close to the next,
No air can pass between them.
Each is joined to the next;
They grasp each other and cannot be pulled apart. (12–17)

'His sneezes are flashes of lightning,
His eyes like the eyelids of the dawn.
From his mouth flaming torches come,
Sparks of fire escape!
From his nostrils issues smoke,
Like steam from a cauldron, or smoke from burning
   rushes!
His breath sets coals ablaze,
And flames burn from his mouth.
Strength lodges in his neck.

Before him dances dismay.
The folds of his skin cling tight,
Cast solid upon him, immovable.
His heart is cast like a stone,
Cast as hard as a lower millstone. (13–24)

'When he rises, the gods are afraid!
When he crashes around, they are beside themselves!
No sword drawn against him will survive,
Nor spear, dart, or javelin.
He treats iron like straw,
Bronze like rotten wood.
No arrow will make him turn and run.
Sling stones for him are turned to chaff.
Clubs are treated like chaff.
He laughs at the rattling of javelins. (25–9)

'His underparts are sharp potsherds;
He drags the mud like a threshing sledge.
He makes the depths boil,
Turns the Sea into a seething pot.
Behind him a shining wake,
Enough to make us think the Deep has white hair!
No-one on the surface of the earth can rule him.
He is made without fear.
He looks down on all the high and mighty.
He is the one who is king over all the sons of pride.' (30–4)

God's Second Speech – Further Comment

These are not the only depictions of Chaos in these speeches of
God. There was another, early on in the first speech, where
God so nearly spoke of the waters of the Sea issuing from her
womb, and then described herself swaddling them, and laying
down the house rules. That Chaos, called simply 'Sea', was
not frightening at all. It was the Chaos of Genesis 1, controlled
by God, put within bounds laid down by him, and rendered
harmless. In Job 38.8–11 Chaos was portrayed as an infant
and a child. Now, in the guise of the Beast and the Dragon, it
has grown to fearful adulthood. It has grown into a monster.

It was made by God, the first of his works. It is not a god, but a creature, like Job. It is part of God's world. There is no dualism here. And yet this Chaos, this Beast, this Dragon, has a life of its own, and seems to enjoy a terrifying degree of freedom. God seems to have untied it and let it loose, just as he set free the wild ass, or the stars of Orion.

Elsewhere in the Old Testament we find talk of God's victory over Leviathan, or over Rahab or Tannin, other names for the same Chaos.

> Rouse yourself! Rouse yourself!
> Put on strength, arm of YHWH!
> Rouse yourself, as in days of old,
> As in the age of long, long ago!
> Was it not you who cut Rahab in pieces,
> Who pierced Tannin through? (Isaiah 51.9)

> You smashed the head of Leviathan,
> gave him as food for the creatures of the desert.
>   (Psalm 74.14)

Such language is drawn from the myth of the slaying of the chaos dragon of the cultures that surrounded Israel. Most famously in Israelite traditions the myth is acted out at the Red Sea, when the waters are split in two, and the dark forces of oppression, played so convincingly by the Pharaoh and his army, are defeated for good. It is buried only a little deeper beneath the Gospel stories of Jesus walking on the back of the Sea, or calming its rages.

There is, however, no mention of triumph in Job 40—1. It would be more comforting if there were, but then Job 40—1 is not concerned with the world as it might be, but the world as it is. Behemoth is not yet cut into pieces; the head of Leviathan is not yet smashed. God can approach Behemoth, with sword drawn for safety's sake (40.19), but that is as far as the poem, and the God of the poem, dare go. Indeed, in this fine speech God seems to get carried away by the extravagance of his words, lost in wonder at the might of these dark forces that seem so utterly fearless, that create in all who meet them such a sense of powerlessness, and cause panic even among the other gods.

Instead of the battlefield, the scene is still largely a domestic one, with talk of lotus flowers, reeds and swamp, the Jordan river, hunting and its weapons, fishing and harpooning, an owner reaching an agreement with a slave, children playing with a pet, traders bartering, steaming cauldrons, smoking rushes, lower millstones, straw, chaff, potsherds, threshing sledges. This remains the world this God inhabits, distancing him yet further from the divine maniac Job imagined before he appeared.

It is not God, it is not YHWH who has been tormenting Job. It is Behemoth and Leviathan. That is surely the meaning of this second speech, or one of them. Job believed with the friends that everything, bad as well as good, came directly from God. They were mistaken. Evil, pain, suffering, oppression, have taken on a life of their own, and far from representing God's ordering of the world, they put it in continual danger. The Beast and the Dragon are the other side of God's creation. There is delight and careful nurturing, to be sure, things assigned and taken to their proper places, food provided even in lean times, mothers delivered safely, and young growing up to be healthy and strong, and excitement and laughter and room for the wonderfully absurd. But that is only one side of the picture, and it is not the side that Job has seen for a very long time. Ever since the catastrophes of the Prologue, he has been living in the shadow of the Beast and the Dragon. Now he can see them for what they are. They are not YHWH! And though so seemingly invincible, they are not even divine. They are creatures of God, like him.

He has seen enough. There is no need for YHWH to say any more. Now he knows what kind of God he is dealing with, and he can put a name, or names, to his tormentor also. He has *seen* God. He has seen the powers that threaten him. He has seen the world in which he lives. Understandably, his pain and grief have been distorting his vision. Now God has taken him on a Cook's tour of the universe, of its terrors as well as its delights, and opened his eyes wide. He has led him outside the small tent of his suffering, and put him beneath the stars crying for joy; taken him far out into the desert, to the wild deer and the ostrich; given him the courage to stand for a spell outside the Dragon's lair. It is enough. It is enough.

Job's Final Response – The Recovery of Dignity

Job answered YHWH and said,
  'I know you can do everything;
  No purpose of yours can be thwarted.
  [You said] "Who is this who hides wise counsel, lacking in
    knowledge?"
  Therefore I have spoken,
    when I did not understand;
  Of things too wonderful for me,
    when I did not know.
  [You said] "Listen, I pray, and I will speak.
  I will question you.
  You supply me with knowledge."
  By the hearing of the ear I had heard of you.
  But now my eye has seen you.
  Therefore I withdraw my case,
  And put my dust and ashes behind me.' (42.1–6)

'I know you can do everything' might seem a strange response to
God's speech about the Beast and the Dragon. That poem only
made clear what God is up against. Is Job speaking, then, with
his tongue in his cheek? Not necessarily. God's speeches have
put things into perspective for him. At last the source of his
plight is clear. He can name the demons, and terrifying though
they are, they have been effectively cut down to size. No longer
is the whole world at the mercy of a divine tyrant run wild. His
own suffering no longer fills his horizons. God does. He had
only heard about him by the hearing of the ear. He knows that
now. Everything he once believed seems now so inadequate, or
so misguided. All his accusations against God were entirely mis-
placed. He has seen God. He has *seen* him! 'You can do everything' is the only thing he can say.

It is not a servile response. The rest of his speech makes that
plain. Twice, not entirely accurately, he quotes God's speeches
(see 38.2–3; 40.7). 'By citing these quotations from Yahweh's
speeches, Job is making it quite explicit', explains Norman
Habel, 'that he is responding formally to the challenge of
Yahweh as his adversary.'[30] Formally, publicly, he withdraws

his case. He was wrong, out of his depth. Yet he is not humiliated. How could he possibly be humiliated by the rare privilege of seeing a God who made the stars of the morning cry out their joy, and who has been so candid in his portrayal of the struggle he has in maintaining the beauty, order and goodness in his creation? Some translators of 42.6 speak of Job ending up despising himself. He does not do so, and increasingly commentators are arguing the Hebrew of that verse cannot sustain that sense in any case.[31] Far from belittling him, this bright vision of God has restored his dignity. He turns his back not on himself, but on his ash heap, his isolation, his shame.

The Epilogue – Another Mixture of the Playful and the Serious

And there the poetry ends, though the book continues for a few verses more. The writer reverts to the playful prose with which he began his great work, and takes us back to never-never land, where Job ends up with twice the perfect number of animals he had at the beginning, and another seven sons and three daughters (as if his earlier children could be replaced!), where the daughters are given the names Turtle Dove, Perfume, and Eye-Shadow, and where, against all the norms of the times and beyond the requirements of the Torah, they are given an inheritance along with their brothers!

Yet, like the Prologue, this short Epilogue also contains the serious. For the first and the last time God turns to the friends: 'I am angry with you and your two friends,' he says to Eliphaz, 'for you have not spoken of me what is right, as my servant Job has' (42.7; see also verse 8). On the face of it the last phrase of this statement, 'as my servant Job has', is astonishing. Surely it is not just a reference to the response Job has just made. Surely God has not forgotten the things Job said to him and about him in his earlier speeches. What he must be upholding here is Job's integrity, his speaking from the heart, his speaking out his pain, his refusal to pretend, to be subservient, to say all the things that 'correct' piety and belief would demand. And what he must be condemning in the friends is their frightened piety, their fabrications, their putting dogma before people, as well as the terms of their 'orthodox' theology and their under-standing of suffering.

He tells the friends to offer sacrifices; Job will be their priest, and will pray for them not to get their just deserts. That prayer is duly offered (42.10), and is a mark of the end of Job's long ordeal and the restoration of his dignity. It is also a sign of his true goodness, for after what the friends have been saying to him, to intercede for them is indeed a noble act.

So ends the long work of Job, and our book, too, is done. We go on our way, after that Epilogue at the end of Job, with a smile on our face, but, more importantly, with that remarkable vision of God and his world filling our eyes, and those words of Job still ringing in our ears:

'By the hearing of the ear I had heard of you.
But now my eye has seen you.'

Notes

1 The Fire of God, and Much Talk

1. James Nohrnberg, *Like unto Moses: The Constituting of an Interpretation* (Indiana University Press, 1995), p. 15.
2. Charles Isbell, 'The Structures of Exodus 1—14', in D. J. A. Clines, D. M. Gunn, A. J. Hauser (eds), *Art and Meaning* (JSOT Press, 1982), p. 42.
3. Nohrnberg, *Like unto Moses*, p. 174.
4. See Trevor Dennis, *Looking God in the Eye: Encountering God in Genesis* (SPCK, 1998), pp. 14–15.
5. See R. P. Carroll, 'Strange Fire: Abstract of Presence Absent in the Text: Meditations on Exodus 3', *JSOT* 61 (1994), p. 43.
6. D. Moody, 'Shekinah', in *The Interpreter's Dictionary of the Bible*, vol. IV (Abingdon Press, 1962), p. 317b.
7. See Othmar Keel, *The Symbolism of the Biblical World: Ancient Near Eastern Iconography and the Book of Psalms* (SPCK, 1978), p. 187.
8. See Carroll, 'Strange Fire', p. 44.
9. I have myself developed this interpretation in my story, 'The Burning Bush', in Dennis, *Imagining God: Stories from Creation to Heaven* (SPCK, 1997), pp. 15–18.
10. See Carroll, 'Strange Fire', p. 45.
11. See 'Strange Fire', p. 45.
12. Everett Fox, *These are the Names: A New English Rendition of the Book of Exodus* (Schocken Books, 1986), p. 26, and reproduced in his *The Five Books of Moses* (The Harvill Press, 1995), p. 273.
13. Carroll, 'Strange Fire', p. 47.
14. *Pace* Carroll, 'Strange Fire', p. 47.
15. See George W. Coats, *Moses: Heroic Man, Man of God* (JSOT Press, 1988), pp. 68–9.
16. See Dennis, *Looking God in the Eye*, ch. 4.

2 Plain Speaking

1. See Dennis, *Looking God in the Eye*, p. 60.
2. I have explored the way in which the stories of the wilderness are developed and turned into tragedy in Dennis, *Lo and Behold! The Power of Old Testament Storytelling* (SPCK, 1991), ch. 4.
3. R. N. Whybray, 'The Immorality of God: Reflections on some passages in Genesis, Job, Exodus and Numbers', *JSOT* 72 (1996), p. 114.
4. Hosea 11.3a and part of verse 4, with the translation of Helen Schüngel Straumann, 'God as Mother in Hosea 11', in Athalya Brenner (ed.), *A Feminist Companion to the Latter Prophets* (Sheffield Academic Press, 1995), pp. 195–6.
5. For discussion of such maternal imagery for God, and of these very passages, see Phyllis Trible, *God and the Rhetoric of Sexuality* (Fortress Press, 1978), ch. 3.
6. I have discussed this part of the episode in greater detail in *Lo and Behold!*, pp. 70–1.
7. Whybray, 'The Immorality of God', p. 116.
8. 'The Immorality of God', p. 115.

3 Another Go-between

1. See p. 122.
2. See p. 125.
3. Nohrnberg, *Like unto Moses*, p. 36.
4. The language of the parting of the Red Sea has clear connections with the creation myths of the ancient Near East. We might say the author of Exodus has demythologized his source material, but the links remain significant.
5. For a discussion of this important aspect of Ezekiel's theology, see Paul Joyce, *Divine Initiative and Human Response in Ezekiel* (JSOT Press, 1989), pp. 97–103.
6. Nohrnberg, *Like unto Moses*, p. 57.
7. See my discussion of this episode in Dennis, *Lo and Behold!*, pp. 76–8.

4 So Near! So Near! Yet so Far!

1. See Deuteronomy 34.10.
2. See R. W. L. Moberly, *At the Mountain of God: Story and Theology in Exodus 32—34*, (JSOT Press, 1983), p. 69.

3. See Numbers 2.17. Brevard S. Childs, *Exodus* (OTL Commentary, SCM, 1974), p. 590, believes there are two distinct traditions about the Tent of Meeting beneath the text of Exodus, one placing it in the middle of the camp, the other outside its bounds. Even if that is true, the text as we have it combines them, and creates its own tensions and pathos as a result. We cannot help but find it significant that in Exodus 33 the Tent is outside, not inside the camp.
4. Moberly, *At the Mountain of God*, pp. 70–1.
5. See Moberly, *At the Mountain of God*, p. 74, who is very clear on this matter.
6. Once again I am indebted to Moberly's sharp eye: *At the Mountain of God*, p. 75.
7. See above, p. 37 (and see also p. 40).
8. Compare Exodus 32.20 with Numbers 5.11–31.
9. See Moberly, *At the Mountain of God*, p. 68.
10. We have already come across a version of this description of God, in Numbers 14.18 (see above, p. 40).
11. Many translations speak of God's back, but, as Moberly points out (*At the Mountain of God*, p. 82), the usual Hebrew term for the back is avoided, and as a result I prefer the vagueness of a word like 'retreating'.
12. Nohrnberg, *Like unto Moses*, p. 351, n. 6.
13. *Like unto Moses*, p. 36.
14. See my discussion in Dennis, *Lo and Behold!*, p. 79.

5 Hello, Hello, Hello! What's Going On Here, Then?

1. See Athalya Brenner, *The Israelite Woman* (JSOT Press, 1985), ch. 5.
2. Karel van der Toorn, *From her Cradle to her Grave: The Role of Religion in the Life of the Israelite and Babylonian Woman* (JSOT Press, 1994), p. 82.
3. For a discussion of the origins of this material, see A. Brenner and F. van Dijk-Hemmes, *On Gendering Texts: Female and Male Voices in the Hebrew Bible* (E. J. Brill, 1993). They do not consider the Shiphrah and Puah story (though I raise the question about its origins myself in *Sarah Laughed: Women's Voices in the Old Testament* (SPCK, 1994), p. 94), nor Judges 13. My own list of biblical books or passages, which is heavily indebted to their work, only covers material whose characteristics suggest it originated

in women's circles. I have not listed speeches put in the mouths of female characters (some of which reveal, of course, a good deal about the functions and position of women in ancient Israelite society).

4. See Yairah Amit, 'Manoah Promptly Followed his Wife (Judges 13.11): On the Place of the Woman in Birth Narratives', in Athalya Brenner (ed.), *A Feminist Companion to Judges* (Sheffield Academic Press, 1993), p. 147.
5. J. Cheryl Exum, *Fragmented Women: Feminist (Sub)versions of Biblical Narratives* (JSOT Press, 1993), pp. 63–8.
6. Adele Reinhartz, 'Samson's Mother: An Unnamed Protagonist', in Brenner (ed.), *A Feminist Companion to Judges*, pp. 157–70 (see especially, pp. 168–9).
7. See Reinhartz, 'Samson's Mother', p. 162, n. 1.
8. See 'Samson's Mother', p. 166.
9. 'Samson's Mother', pp. 166–8.
10. Lillian R. Klein, *The Triumph of Irony in the Book of Judges* (The Almond Press, 1988), pp. 111–14.
11. David E. Bynum, 'Samson as a Biblical Φὴρ ὀρεσκῷος', in Susan Niditch (ed.), *Text and Tradition: The Hebrew Bible and Folklore* (Scholars Press, 1990), p. 60.
12. See Reinhartz, 'Samson's Mother', p. 167; Klein, *The Triumph of Irony*, pp. 113–14.
13. See Alberto Soggin's comment on that verse in *Judges* (OTL Commentary, SCM, 1981), p. 241.
14. The text does not tell us where this first meeting takes place, but in the absence of any information, and in the light of the story's being careful to locate the second encounter out in the open, it would seem most natural to speak of the women's quarters in Eluma's and Manoah's house.
15. I am indebted for this interpretation of Manoah's invitation to David M. Gunn, and Danna Nolan Fewell, *Narrative in the Hebrew Bible* (Oxford University Press, 1993), p. 66.
16. The Hebrew of the last part of the verse is obscure and possibly corrupt. Our translation is close to that of the Jewish Bible, or Tanakh, which has, 'a marvellous thing happened while Manoah and his wife looked on', but it is by no means certain.

6 Now my Eye has Seen You

1. Martin Buber, *The Prophetic Faith* (Harper and Row, 1960), p. 196.
2. Athalya Brenner, 'Job the Pious? The Characterization of Job in the Narrative Framework of the Book', *JSOT* 43 (1989), pp. 37–52. My treatment of the Prologue to Job owes a great deal to Brenner's insights.
3. Job 7.17–18 parodies Psalm 8.4; Job 9.5–10 and 12.7–25 parody hymns of praise such as Psalms 104 or 107; Job 9.30–1 parodies Psalm 51.9; Job 10.2–7, 19.22 and especially 23.8–9 parody the sentiments of Psalm 139.7–12; Job 10.8–15 parodies such passages as Psalm 139.13–16, or Jeremiah 1.4; Job 14.5–6 parodies Psalm 55.6–7. For most of these references I am indebted to Katharine Dell, *Shaking a Fist at God: Understanding Suffering through the Book of Job* (HarperCollins, 1995), pp. 47–50.
4. Brenner, 'Job the Pious?', p. 40.
5. See David J. A. Clines, *Job 1—20* (Word Biblical Commentary, Word Books, 1989), p. 10.
6. Brenner, 'Job the Pious?', pp. 43–4, and p. 50, n. 14.
7. The notion of the patient Job is, in fact, found in our Bibles, at James 5.11. Katharine Dell gives examples of music, painting and drama on Job which take note of the Prologue and the Epilogue of 42.7–17, and ignore the rest of the work: Dell, *Shaking a Fist*, pp. 25–6.
8. Ellen van Wolde, *Mr and Mrs Job* (SCM, 1997), pp. 20–3, quotes passages in the Septuagint (the Greek version of the OT, written in the third century BCE), and the rabbinic work of the second century BCE, the *Testament of Job*, which begin to explore the pain of Job's wife, and to speak of *her* misery.
9. David J. A. Clines has exposed its misogyny in his book, *Interested Parties: The Ideology of Writers and Readers of the Hebrew Bible* (Sheffield Academic Press, 1995), pp. 128–9.
10. Norman C. Habel, *The Book of Job* (OTL Commentary, SCM, 1985), p. 39.
11. Habel, *The Book of Job*, p. 40.
12. Buber, *The Prophetic Faith*, p. 189.
13. Robert Davidson has written powerfully on the subject of Eliphaz's speeches in *The Courage to Doubt* (SCM, 1983), pp. 177–9.
14. Buber, *The Prophetic Faith*, p. 189.
15. Habel, *The Book of Job*, pp. 54–7; for more detailed comment, see

the discussion of the passages concerned in the body of the commentary.

16. The interpretation of both those passages is not easy. David Clines argues that the 'witness' is Job's own testimony, left on record in heaven to put the case for his innocence (*Job 1—20*, pp. 389–90, 458–9). Norman Habel thinks Job is envisaging an angelic figure, a counterpart to the Satan of the Prologue, a figure who will defend rather than accuse, and who, as a member of YHWH's court, will be listened to (*The Book of Job*, pp. 275–6, 305–7).

17. Leo G. Perdue, *Wisdom and Creation: The Theology of Wisdom Literature* (Abingdon Press, 1994), p. 165.

18. Perdue, *Wisdom and Creation*, p. 163.

19. *Wisdom and Creation*, p. 164.

20. There has long been debate among scholars about whether Elihu's speeches were part of the original work, or were added by a later hand. Differences of opinion remain, and are likely to continue to do so.

21. As we mentioned earlier, the author of Job employs a number of archaic names for God, names, that is, that must have seemed archaic to his original audience. 'Shaddai', often translated, 'The Almighty', is one of them. It is a name that seems to be designed to convey a sense of God's mystery and raw power.

22. Martin Buber, *The Prophetic Faith*, p. 196, observes: 'It is clear that this God, Who answers from the tempest, is different from the God of the Prologue.'

23. This passage is presented as a rehearsal of what Job will say to God when he appears, but Job's passion takes over, and it quickly turns to prayer. Job is not just rehearsing here. He is playing it for real.

24. There are a few verses in this speech of God's and the next that are problematic and where no translation can be certain. I have not indicated them in my own translation, since I am careful to avoid hanging any arguments upon them, when I come to comment on the text. The more detailed commentaries, such as Habel's, indicate where the difficulties lie.

25. Another of the archaic names used of God. In the book of Job it occurs forty-one times. Elsewhere in the OT it is rare.

26. See also the forceful attacks on idolatry in Isaiah 40.18–20; 41.7; 44.9–20; 46.5–7.

27. See above, pp. 24–5.

28. Another of the archaic names for God employed by the poet.
29. See, for example, Habel, *The Book of Job*, pp. 557–61; Perdue, *Wisdom and Creation*, p. 177. Robert Fyall, *How Does God Treat his Friends?* (Christian Focus Publications, 1995), p. 119, argues that Behemoth is an embodiment not only of chaos and evil, but also of death.
30. Habel, *The Book of Job*, p. 581.
31. See Habel, *The Book of Job*, pp. 582–3; Perdue, *Wisdom and Creation*, pp. 181, 364 n. 120; van Wolde, *Mr and Mrs Job*, pp. 136–7.

References

Amit, Yairah, 'Manoah Promptly Followed his Wife (Judges 13.11): On the Place of the Woman in Birth Narratives', in Athalya Brenner (ed.), *A Feminist Companion to Judges*, Sheffield Academic Press, 1993

Brenner, Athalya, *The Israelite Woman*, JSOT Press, 1985

Brenner, Athalya, 'Job the Pious? The Characterization of Job in the Narrative Framework of the Book', *JSOT* 43 (1989)

Brenner, A., and F. van Dijk-Hemmes, *On Gendering Texts: Female and Male Voices in the Hebrew Bible*, E. J. Brill, 1993

Buber, Martin, *The Prophetic Faith*, Harper and Row, 1960

Bynum, David E., 'Samson as a Biblical Φὴρ ὀρεσκῷος', in Susan Niditch (ed.), *Text and Tradition: The Hebrew Bible and Folklore*, Scholars Press, 1990

Carroll, R. P., 'Strange Fire: Abstract of Presence Absent in the Text: Meditations on Exodus 3', *JSOT* 61 (1994)

Childs, Brevard S., *Exodus*, OTL Commentary, SCM, 1974

Clines, David J. A., *Interested Parties: The Ideology of Writers and Readers of the Hebrew Bible*, Sheffield Academic Press, 1995

Clines, David J. A., *Job 1—20*, Word Biblical Commentary, Word Books, 1989

Coats, George W., *Moses: Heroic Man, Man of God*, JSOT Press, 1988

Davidson, Robert, *The Courage to Doubt*, SCM, 1983

Dell, Katharine, *Shaking a Fist at God: Understanding Suffering through the Book of Job*, HarperCollins, 1995

Dennis, Trevor, *Lo and Behold! The Power of Old Testament Storytelling*, SPCK, 1991

Dennis, Trevor, *Sarah Laughed: Women's Voices in the Old Testament*, SPCK, 1994

Dennis, Trevor, *Imagining God: Stories from Creation to Heaven*, SPCK, 1997

Exum, J. Cheryl, *Fragmented Women: Feminist (Sub)versions of Biblical Narratives*, JSOT Press, 1993

Fox, Everett, *The Five Books of Moses*, The Harvill Press, 1995
Fox, Everett, *These are the Names: A New English Rendition of the Book of Exodus*, Schocken Books, 1986
Fyall, Robert, *How Does God Treat his Friends?*, Christian Focus Publications, 1995
Gunn, David M., and Danna Nolan Fewell, *Narrative in the Hebrew Bible*, Oxford University Press, 1993
Habel, Norman C., *The Book of Job*, OTL Commentary, SCM, 1985
Isbell, Charles, 'The Structures of Exodus 1—14', in D. J. A. Clines, D. M. Gunn and A. J. Hauser (eds), *Art and Meaning*, JSOT Press, 1982
Joyce, Paul, *Divine Initiative and Human Response in Ezekiel*, JSOT Press, 1989
Keel, Othmar, *The Symbolism of the Biblical World: Ancient Near Eastern Iconography and the Book of Psalms*, SPCK, 1978
Klein, Lillian R., *The Triumph of Irony in the Book of Judges*, Almond Press, 1988
Moberly, R. W. L., *At the Mountain of God: Story and Theology in Exodus 32—34*, JSOT Press, 1983
Moody, D., 'Shekinah', in *The Interpreter's Dictionary of the Bible*, vol. IV, Abingdon Press, 1962
Nohrnberg, James, *Like unto Moses: The Constituting of an Interpretation*, Indiana University Press, 1995
Perdue, Leo G., *Wisdom and Creation: The Theology of Wisdom Literature*, Abingdon Press, 1994
Reinhartz, Adele, 'Samson's Mother: An Unnamed Protagonist', in Athalya Brenner (ed.), *A Feminist Companion to Judges*, Sheffield Academic Press, 1993
Soggin, Alberto, *Judges*, OTL Commentary, SCM, 1981
Straumann, Helen Schüngel, 'God as Mother in Hosea 11', in Athalya Brenner (ed.), *A Feminist Companion to the Latter Prophets*, Sheffield Academic Press, 1995
Toorn, Karel van der, *From her Cradle to her Grave: The Role of Religion in the Life of the Israelite and Babylonian Woman*, JSOT Press, 1994
Trible, Phyllis, *God and the Rhetoric of Sexuality*, Fortress Press, 1978
Whybray, R. N., 'The Immorality of God: Reflections on some Passages in Genesis, Job, Exodus and Numbers', *JSOT* 72 (1996)
Wolde, Ellen van, *Mr and Mrs Job*, SCM, 1997

Index

121

manna 21–2
Manoah ix, 67–71; his wife, *see* Eluma
Mary of Magdala 57
Mary of Nazareth 57
messenger of God 45, 59, 63, 65
Midian 2–3, 19
Miriam 56
Moses ix, xiii–xiv; at the Burning Bush 1–16; as friend of God 2, 26, 34–5; his objections to God's call 7–13, 16; anger with God 18–19, 22–3; loneliness of his office 24; as go-between 28–9, 44; called to be progenitor of a nation 36–9; appeals to God's honour 39; pleads for God's forgiveness of the people 41, 43; destroys the Golden Calf 42; intercedes again and finds favour with God 46–50; asks to see God's glory 50–2; dies 53–5
motherhood of God 24–5, 98–9
mystery of God 30

natural world 99
Noadiah 56
Noah 34, 47

Palestine 12
patience of Job 78
Pharaoh 2, 3, 12, 13, 17, 18
Philistines 59, 66

prayer 27; of anger 20–1; of lament and complaint 23; *see also under* Moses *and* Job
Promised Land *see* Canaan
Puah 59

Rahab 59

Samson 63, 66; identity of his father 63–4
Samuel 59
Shiphrah 59
Sinai 4, 5, 29
Sodom 15
sovereignty of God 51
staff, Moses' 16
suffering 107; of Job 81, 100

Ten Commandments 29
Tent of Meeting 29, 45–6
theophany 28, 50–2
Torah xiii, 28, 31

wealth 77
women: encounter with God in the Bible xv, 56–7; voices in biblical literature 58, 61; subject to their husbands 69
wrath of God 15

YHWH: name of God xv–xvi, 10, 52

Zlelponith 61
Zophar 84

Bible Reference Index

The Society for Promoting Christian Knowledge (SPCK) was founded in 1698. It has as its purpose three main tasks:

- **Communicating the Christian faith in its rich diversity**
- **Helping people to understand the Christian faith and to develop their personal faith**
- **Equipping Christians for mission and ministry**

SPCK Worldwide serves the Church through Christian literature and communication projects in over 100 countries. Special schemes also provide books for those training for ministry in many parts of the developing world. SPCK Worldwide's ministry involves Churches of many traditions. This worldwide service depends upon the generosity of others and all gifts are spent wholly on ministry programmes, without deductions.

SPCK Bookshops support the life of the Christian community by making available a full range of Christian literature and other resources, and by providing support to bookstalls and book agents throughout the UK. SPCK Bookshops' mail order department meets the needs of overseas customers and those unable to have access to local bookshops.

SPCK Publishing produces Christian books and resources, covering a wide range of inspirational, pastoral, practical and academic subjects. Authors are drawn from many different Christian traditions, and publications aim to meet the needs of a wide variety of readers in the UK and throughout the world.

The Society does not necessarily endorse the individual views contained in its publications, but hopes they stimulate readers to think about and further develop their Christian faith.

For further information about the Society, please write to:
SPCK, Holy Trinity Church, Marylebone Road,
London NW1 4DU, United Kingdom.
Telephone: 0171 387 5282